500 FACTS

History

500 FACTS

History

:itles

2 4 6 8 10 9 7 5 3 1

Editorial Director Belinda Gallagher
Art Director Jo Brewer
Editions Manager Bethan Ellish
Cover Designer Simon Lee
Designers Joe Jones, Sally Lace, Louisa Leitao, Elaine Wilkinson
Editors Rosie McGuire, Sarah Parkin
Indexer Eleanor Holme
Production Manager Elizabeth Brunwin
Reprographics Stephan Davis, Lorraine King, Ian Paulyn
Contributors Fiona Macdonald, John Malam, Rupert Matthews,
Dan North, Richard Tames, Philip Steele, Jane Walker

ISBN 978-1-84810-166-1

Printed in China

British Library Cataloguing-in-Publication Data
A catalogue record for this book is available from the British Library

Made with paper from a sustainable forest

www.mileskelly.net
info@mileskelly.net

www.factsforprojects.com
The one-stop homework helper —
pictures, facts, videos, projects and more

Contents

GLADIATORS 92–133

MUMMIES 134–175

The heart of ancient Egypt

1 **Without the waters of the river Nile, the amazing civilization of ancient Egypt might never have existed.** The Nile provided water for drinking and for watering crops. Every year its floods left a strip of rich dark soil on both sides of the river. Farmers grew their crops in these fertile strips. The Egyptians called their country Kemet, which means 'black land', after this dark soil. The Nile was also important for transport, it was a trade route for the Egyptians.

▼ The Nile supported many activities of ancient Egypt such as trade and farming, it was an important water source.

Royal news

2 **The rulers of ancient Egypt were called pharaohs.** The word 'pharaoh' means great house. The pharaoh was the most important and powerful person in the country. Many people believed he was a god.

3 **Ramses II ruled for over 60 years.** He was the only pharaoh to carry the title 'the Great' after his name. Ramses was a great builder and a brave soldier. He was also the father of an incredibly large number of children: 96 boys and 60 girls.

Ramses II

▶ Here the pharaoh is holding the symbols of his rule, the hook and flail. Workers used these tools to separate grain from the stalks.

▼ These people are paying tribute to the pharaoh. This means that they have come from the surrounding countries to give him presents and tell him how great he is!

▲ On her wedding day, the bride wore a long linen dress or tunic.

4 **The pharaoh often married a close female relative, such as his sister or half-sister.** In this way the blood of the royal family remained pure. The title of 'pharaoh' was usually passed on to the eldest son of the pharaoh's most important wife.

5 **Officials called viziers helped the pharaoh to govern Egypt.** Each ruler appointed two viziers – one each for Upper and Lower Egypt. Viziers were powerful men. Each vizier was in charge of a number of royal overseers. Each overseer was responsible for a particular area of government, for example the army or granaries where the grain was stored. The pharaoh, though, was in charge of everyone.

6 **Over 30 different dynasties ruled ancient Egypt.** A dynasty is a line of rulers from the same family.

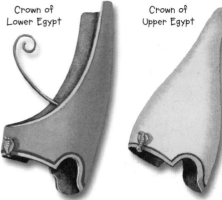

Crown of Lower Egypt

Crown of Upper Egypt

▲ The double crown of Egypt was made up of two crowns, the bucket-shaped red crown of Lower Egypt and the bottle-shaped white crown of Upper Egypt.

▲ This vizier is checking the sacks of grain that have been brought in from the harvest while a criminal awaits his punishment. The viziers of ancient Egypt were among the most important people in the country.

Magnificent monuments

7 The three pyramids at the town of Giza are more than 4500 years old. They were built for three kings: Khufu, Khafre and Menkaure. The biggest, the Great Pyramid, took more than 20 years to build. Around 4000 stonemasons and thousands of other workers were needed to complete the job.

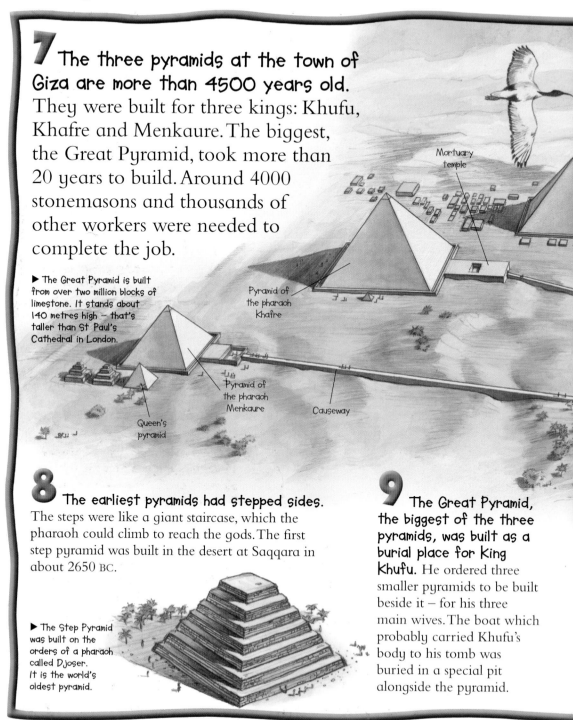

▶ The Great Pyramid is built from over two million blocks of limestone. It stands about 140 metres high – that's taller than St Paul's Cathedral in London.

Mortuary temple

Pyramid of the pharaoh Khafre

Pyramid of the pharaoh Menkaure

Causeway

Queen's pyramid

8 The earliest pyramids had stepped sides. The steps were like a giant staircase, which the pharaoh could climb to reach the gods. The first step pyramid was built in the desert at Saqqara in about 2650 BC.

▶ The Step Pyramid was built on the orders of a pharaoh called Djoser. It is the world's oldest pyramid.

9 The Great Pyramid, the biggest of the three pyramids, was built as a burial place for King Khufu. He ordered three smaller pyramids to be built beside it – for his three main wives. The boat which probably carried Khufu's body to his tomb was buried in a special pit alongside the pyramid.

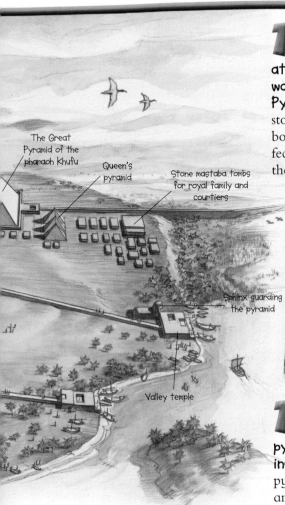

The Great Pyramid of the pharaoh Khufu

Queen's pyramid

Stone mastaba tombs for royal family and courtiers

Sphinx guarding the pyramid

Valley temple

10 The Great Sphinx at Giza guards the way to the Great Pyramid. It is a huge stone statue with the body of a lion and the head of a human. The features on the face were carved to look like the pharaoh Khafre.

I DON'T BELIEVE IT!

A special handbook for tomb robbers called 'The Book of Buried Pearls' gave details of hidden treasures and tips for sneaking past the spirits that guarded the dead!

11 Tomb robbers broke into the pyramids to steal the fabulous treasures inside. To make things difficult for the robbers, pyramid builders added heavy doors of granite and built false corridors inside the pyramids.

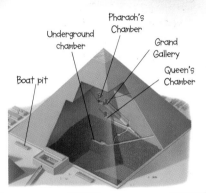

Pharaoh's Chamber

Underground chamber

Grand Gallery

Queen's Chamber

Boat pit

12 Inside the Great Pyramid were two large burial rooms, one each for the pharaoh and queen. The Pharaoh's Chamber was reached by a corridor called the Grand Gallery, with a roof more than 8 metres above the floor, four times higher than a normal ceiling. Once the king's body was inside the burial chamber, the entrance was sealed with stone blocks. The last workers had to leave by specially built escape passages.

Supreme beings

13 **The ancient Egyptians worshipped more than 1000 different gods and goddesses.** The most important god of all was Ra, the sun god. People believed that he was swallowed up each evening by the sky goddess Nut. During the night Ra travelled through the underworld and was born again each morning.

◄ The sun god Ra later became Amun-Ra. He was combined with another god to make a new king of the gods.

14 **A god was often shown as an animal, or as half-human, half-animal.** Sobek was a god of the river Nile. Crocodiles were kept in pools next to Sobek's temples. Bastet was the goddess of cats, musicians and dancers. The cat was a sacred animal in ancient Egypt. When a pet cat died, the body would be wrapped and laid in a cat-shaped coffin before burial in the city's cat cemetery. The moon god Thoth usually had the head of an ibis, but he was sometimes shown as a baboon. The ancient Egyptians believed that hieroglyphic writing came from Thoth.

▼ Some of the well known gods that were represented by animals.

Sobek   Bastet   Thoth

15 As god of the dead, Osiris was in charge of the underworld. Ancient Egyptians believed that dead people travelled to the kingdom of the underworld below the Earth. Osiris and his wife Isis were the parents of the god Horus, protector of the pharaoh.

Isis　　Osiris　　Horus

16 Anubis was in charge of preparing bodies to be mummified. This work was known as embalming. Because jackals were often found near cemeteries, Anubis, who watched over the dead, was given the form of a jackal. Egyptian priests often wore Anubis masks when preparing mummies.

QUIZ

1. Who was buried inside the Great Pyramid?
2. Describe the crown of Upper Egypt.
3. What was a vizier?
4. Which pharaoh ruled for more than 90 years?
5. What is the Great Sphinx?

Answers:
1. King Khufu 2. A bottle-shaped white crown 3. An important governor 4. Pepi II 5. An animal with the body of a lion and the head of a human

17 A pharaoh called Amenhotep IV changed his name to Akhenaten, after the sun god Aten. During his reign Akhenaten made Aten the king of all the gods.

▼ Anubis preparing a body for mummification.

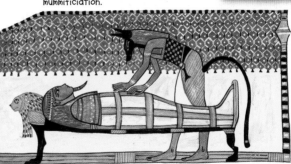

In tombs and temples

18 From about 2150 BC pharaohs were not buried in pyramids, but in tombs in the Valley of the Kings. At that time it was a fairly remote place, surrounded by steep cliffs lying on the west bank of the Nile opposite the city of Thebes. Some of the tombs were cut into the cliffside, others were built deep underground.

▲ Robbers looted everything from the royal tombs – gold, silver, precious stones, furniture, clothing, pots – sometimes they even stole the dead ruler's body!

19 Like the pyramids, the riches in the royal tombs attracted robbers. The entrance to the Valley of the Kings was guarded, but robbers had broken into every tomb except one within 1000 years. The only one they missed was the tomb of the boy king Tutankhamun, and even this had been partially robbed and re-sealed.

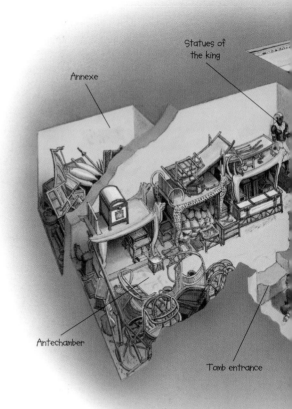

Statues of the king

Annexe

Antechamber

Tomb entrance

▲ The solid gold death mask of Tutankhamun found in the Valley of the Kings. The young king's tomb was discovered, with its contents untouched, about 80 years ago.

20 Archaeologist Howard Carter discovered the tomb of Tutankhamun in 1922. An archaeologist is someone who searches for historical objects. Tutankhamun's body was found inside a nest of three mummy cases in a sarcophagus (stone coffin). The sarcophagus was inside a set of four wooden shrines big enough to contain a modern car.

I DON'T BELIEVE IT!

Temple visitors had to shave off their hair and eyebrows before they were allowed to enter the sacred buildings.

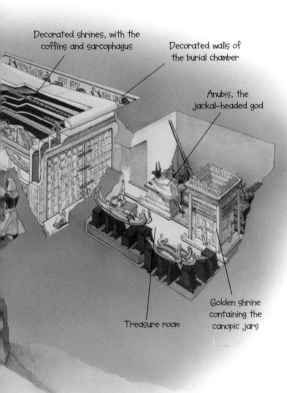

Decorated shrines, with the coffins and sarcophagus

Decorated walls of the burial chamber

Anubis, the jackal-headed god

Golden shrine containing the canopic jars

Treasure room

▲ Carter, and his sponsor Lord Carnarvon, finally found Tutankhamun's tomb after five years of archaeological exploration in Egypt. Carnarvon died just four months after he first entered the tomb. Some people said he was the victim of Tutankhamun's 'curse' because he had disturbed the pharaoh's body. In fact Carnarvon died from an infected mosquito bite.

21 The ancient Egyptians built fabulous temples to worship their gods. Powerful priests ruled over the temples, and the riches and lands attached to them. Many of the finest temples were dedicated to Amun-Ra, king of the gods.

22 The temple at Abu Simbel, in the south of Egypt, is carved out of sandstone rock. It was built on the orders of Ramses II. The temple was built in such a way that on two days each year (22 February and 22 October) the Sun's first rays shine on the back of the inner room, lighting up statues of the gods.

▲ Four enormous statues of Ramses II, each over 20 metres high, guard the temple entrance at Abu Simbel.

Big building blocks!

23 Each block used to build the Great Pyramid weighed as much as two and a half adult elephants! Labourers used copper chisels and saws to cut and shape the stones before dragging them on wooden sledges to the base of the pyramid.

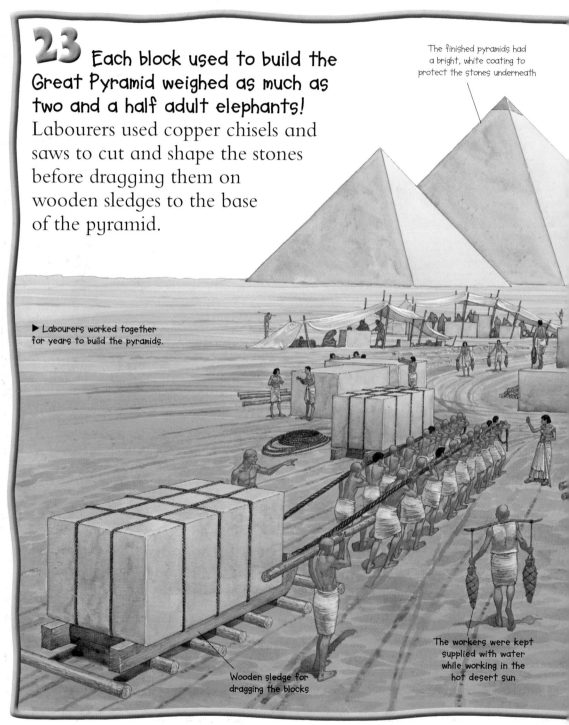

The finished pyramids had a bright, white coating to protect the stones underneath

▶ Labourers worked together for years to build the pyramids.

Wooden sledge for dragging the blocks

The workers were kept supplied with water while working in the hot desert sun

The huge stones had to be levered into exactly the right position

Up to two million of these blocks could be used to make one pyramid. It could take as long as 20 years

Teams of workers had to drag the stones up the slopes

24 Steep ramps of earth and mud brick were built to raise the stones onto the pyramid structure. As each new layer of stones was laid in position, the ramps were lengthened to allow workers to build the next layer.

I DON'T BELIEVE IT!

Imhotep, the architect of the Step Pyramid at Saqqara, was a busy man – he was also a vizier, a doctor, a scribe, a high priest and a poet! He served under a total of four different kings.

Making mummies

25 **Making a mummy was difficult and skilled work.** First the brain, stomach, lungs and other organs were removed, but the heart was left in place. Next, the body was covered with salts and left to dry for up to 40 days. The dried body was washed and filled with linen and other stuffing to keep its shape. Finally, it was oiled and wrapped in layers of linen bandages.

The priest in charge wore a jackal mask to represent the god Anubis

The organs were stored in canopic jars like these. Each jar represented a god

Amulet placed with the mummy for luck

Mummified dog

Mummified cat

26 **Animals were made into mummies too.** A nobleman might be buried with a mummy of his pet cat. Mummification was expensive, so people only preserved animals in this way to offer them to the gods. One mummified crocodile discovered by archaeologists was over 4.5 metres long!

27 **Body parts were removed from the dead person and stored in special containers.** The stomach, intestines, lungs and liver were cut out and stored in four separate jars, called canopic jars.

Wooden coffin for the body

MAKE A DEATH MASK

You will need:

play mask (made of plastic or stiff card)
PVA glue   paintbrush
newspaper   poster paints
white paint

Use an inexpensive play mask, such as a Halloween one, as your basic mask. Cover the mask with a thick layer of PVA glue. Spread layers of torn newspaper strips over the mask and leave to dry.

Cover the mask with white paint. When dry, use the poster paints to create an amazing death mask of your own! If you haven't got gold-coloured paint, you can use gold glitter to create the same effect.

28 **A mask was fitted over the face of a mummy.** The ancient Egyptians believed that the mask would help the dead person's spirit to recognize the mummy later on. A pharaoh's mummy mask was made of gold and precious stones.

29 **When ready for burial, a mummy was placed inside a special case.** Some cases were simple wooden boxes, but others were shaped like mummies and richly decorated. The mummy case of an important person, such as a pharaoh or a nobleman, was sealed inside a stone coffin called a sarcophagus.

Home sweet home

30 Egyptian houses were made from mud bricks dried in the sun. Mud was taken from the river Nile, and straw and pebbles were added to make it stronger. The trunks of palm trees supported the flat roofs. The inside walls of houses were covered with plaster, and often painted. Wealthy Egyptians lived in large houses with several storeys. A poorer family, though, might live in a crowded single room.

◄ A mixture of mud, straw and stones was poured into wooden frames or shaped into bricks and left to harden in the sun.

31 In most Egyptian homes there was a small shrine. Here, members of the family worshipped their household god.

◄ The dwarf god, Bes, was the ancient Egyptian god of children and the home.

32 Egyptians furnished their homes with wooden stools, chairs, tables, storage chests and carved beds. A low three- or four-legged footstool was one of the most popular items of furniture. Mats of woven reeds covered the floors.

33 Rich families lived in spacious villas in the countryside. A typical villa had a pond filled with fish, a walled garden and an orchard of fruit trees.

▼ Family life in ancient Egypt with children playing board games.

34

They cooked their food in a clay oven or over an open fire. Most kitchens were equipped with a cylinder-shaped oven made from bricks of baked clay. They burned either charcoal or wood as fuel. They cooked food in two-handled pottery saucepans.

QUIZ

1. Why did the Egyptians bury a boat next to their pharaoh?

2. Which part of the body was left inside a mummy?

3. Who was Howard Carter?

4. Why did farmworkers have nothing to do between July and November each year?

Answers:
1. So he can use it in the next life 2. The heart 3. The man who discovered the tomb of Tutankhamun 4. The river Nile had flooded the farmland

35

Pottery lamps provided the lighting in Egyptian homes. They filled the container with oil and burned a wick made of cotton or flax. Houses had very small windows, and sometimes none at all, so there was often very little natural light. Small windows kept out the strong sunlight, helping to keep houses cool.

36

In Egypt it was good to eat with your fingers! In rich households, servants would even bring jugs of water between courses so that people could rinse their hands.

Dressing up

37 **Egyptians wore lucky charms called amulets.** The charms were meant to protect the wearer from evil spirits and to bring good luck. One of the most popular ones was the eye of the god Horus. Children wore amulets shaped like fish to protect them from drowning in the river Nile.

▼ The eye of Horus was thought to protect everything behind it. The god Horus had his eye torn out while defending the throne of Egypt. Later, the eye was magically repaired.

38 **In Egypt, men and women both wore eye make-up.** A special black eye make-up, called kohl, was made from ground-up raw metals mixed with oil. The Egyptians believed it had magical healing powers and could restore bad eyesight and fight eye infections. Egyptians also used face rouge for the cheeks and lips, face powder, paint for fingernails and hair dyes.

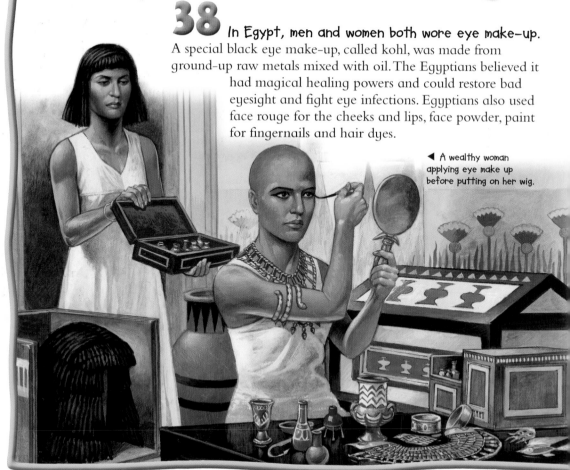

◀ A wealthy woman applying eye make up before putting on her wig.

39 Most clothes were made from light-coloured linen. Women wore long dresses, often with pleated cloaks. Noblewomen's dresses were made of the best cloth with beads sewn onto it. Men wore either robes or kilt-like skirts, a piece of linen wrapped around the waist and tied in a decorative knot.

▶ This fine long dress is worn with a see-through cloak. Clothes like these made sure that the people of Egypt kept cool in the hot weather.

MAKE A MAGIC EYE CHARM

You will need:

self-hardening modelling clay
length of leather strip or thick cord
pencil   poster paints
paintbrush   varnish

1. Knead the clay until soft and then shape into the charm.

2. Add extra clay for the pupil of the eye and at the top of the charm. Use the pencil to make the top piece into a loop.

3. Leave the clay to harden. Paint in bright colours and leave to dry.

4. Varnish, then thread the leather strip or cord through the loop and wear your charm for extra luck.

40 Wealthy people wore wigs made from human hair or sheep's wool which they kept in special boxes on stands at home. Girls wore their hair in pigtails, while boys mostly had shaved heads, sometimes with a plaited lock on one side.

Comb

Hair pins

Comb

Wigs

▲ Wigs were often long and elaborate and needed a lot of attention. Egyptians cared for their wigs with combs made of wood and ivory. They sometimes used curling tongs as well.

41 Sandals were made from papyrus and other reeds. Rich people, courtiers and kings and queens wore padded leather ones. Footwear was a luxury item, and most ordinary people walked around barefoot. Colourful pictures of sandals were even painted onto the feet of mummies!

Leather sandals

Reed sandals

Clever Egyptians

42 **The insides of many Egyptian tombs were decorated with brightly coloured wall paintings.** They often depicted scenes from the dead person's life, showing him or her as a healthy young person. The Egyptians believed that these scenes would come to life in the next world.

Sunken relief

▶ The Egyptians produced raised reliefs by cutting away the background, and sunken relief by cutting stone from inside the outline.

Raised relief

43 **Egyptian sculptors carved enormous stone statues of their pharaohs and gods.** These were often placed outside a tomb or temple to guard the entrance. Scenes, called reliefs, were carved into the walls of temples and tombs. These often showed the person as they were when they were young, enjoying scenes from daily life. This was so that when the god Osiris brought the dead person and the tomb paintings back to life, the tomb owners would have a good time in the afterlife.

44 **The ancient Egyptians had three different calendars: an everyday farming one, an astronomical and a lunar (Moon) calendar.** The 365-day farming calendar was made up of three seasons of four months. The astronomical calendar was based on observations of the star Sirius, which reappeared each year at the start of the flood season. Priests kept a calendar based on the movements of the Moon which told them when to perform ceremonies for to the moon god Khonsu.

▲ The days on this calendar are written in black and red. Black days are ordinary, but the red days are unlucky.

◀ Several artists worked on the tomb paintings. A junior artist drew the outlines of the scene, which were then checked and corrected by a more senior artist. Next, painters filled in the outlines in colour.

45 **Astronomers recorded their observations of the night skies.** The Egyptian calendar was based on the movement of Sirius, the brightest star in the sky. The Egyptians used their knowledge of astronomy to build temples that lined up with certain stars or with the movement of the Sun.

I DON'T BELIEVE IT!

Bulbs of garlic were used to ward off snakes and to get rid of tapeworms from people's bodies.

46 **Egyptian doctors knew how to set broken bones and treat illnesses such as fevers.** They used medicines made from plants such as garlic and juniper to treat sick people. The Egyptians had a good knowledge of the basic workings of the human body.

47 **The Egyptians used a device called a nilometer to measure the depth of the river Nile.** They inserted measuring posts into the riverbed at intervals along the bank so they could check the water levels at the start of each flood season.

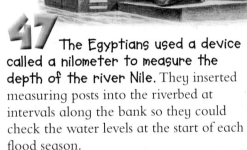

Greece was great

48 **Ancient Greece was a small country, but its people had great ideas.** From around 2000 BC, they created a splendid civilization that reached its peak between 500–400 BC. All citizens contributed to a society that respected people's rights, encouraged the best in human nature and lived in harmony with the natural world. Today, we still admire Greek sport, medicine, drama, politics, poetry and art.

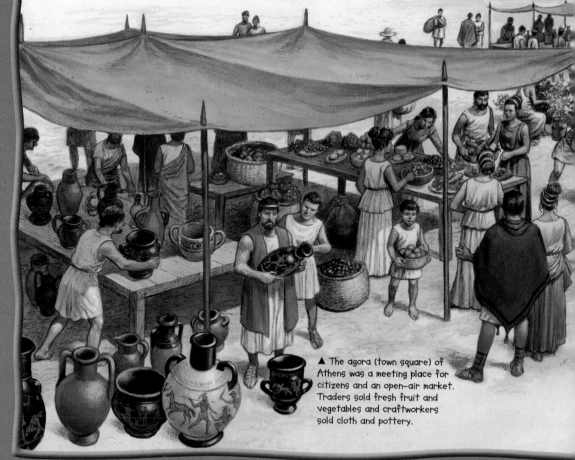

▲ The agora (town square) of Athens was a meeting place for citizens and an open-air market. Traders sold fresh fruit and vegetables and craftworkers sold cloth and pottery.

Steeped in history

49 **The ancient Greeks were proud of their beautiful country.** There were high snowy mountains, swift rushing streams, thick forests, flowery meadows and narrow, fertile plains beside the sea. Around the coast there were thousands of rocky islands, some small and poor, others large and prosperous.

◀ A carved stone figure of a woman found in the Cyclades Islands. The design is very simple but strong and graceful.

▼ This timeline shows some of the important events in the history of ancient Greece.

50 **Greek civilization began on the islands.** Some of the first evidence of farming in Greece comes from the Cyclades Islands. Around 6000 BC, people living there began to plant grain and build villages. They buried their dead in graves filled with treasures, such as carved marble figures, pottery painted with magic sun symbols and gold and silver jewellery.

TIMELINE OF GREECE

c. 40,000 BC
First people in Greece. They are hunters and gatherers

c. 2000–1450 BC
Minoan civilization on the island of Crete

c. 1250 BC
Traditional date of the Trojan War

c. 900–700 BC
Greek civilization grows strong again

c. 6000 BC
First farmers in Greece

c. 1600–1100 BC
Mycenean civilization on mainland Greece

c. 1100–900 BC
A time of decline – kingdoms weaken, writing stops

c. 776 BC
Traditional date of first Olympic Games

◀ This jar, made around 900 BC, is rather dull and plain. It suggests that times were troubled and Greek people had no money to spare for art.

51 Between 1100–900 BC, the history of Greece is a mystery.
From 2000–1100 BC, powerful kings ruled Greece. They left splendid buildings and objects behind them, and used writing. But between around 1100–900 BC, there were no strong kingdoms, little art, few new buildings – and writing disappeared.

▲ Alexander the Great conquered an empire stretching from Greece to India.

52 Migrants settled in distant lands.
By around 700 BC, Greece was overcrowded. There were too many people, not enough farmland to grow food and some islands were short of water. Greek families left to set up colonies far away, from southern France to North Africa, Turkey and Bulgaria.

53 When the neighbours invaded, Greek power collapsed.
After 431 BC, Greek cities were at war and the fighting weakened them. In 338 BC, Philip II of Macedonia (a kingdom north of Greece) invaded with a large army. After Philip died, his son, Alexander the Great, made Greece part of his mighty empire.

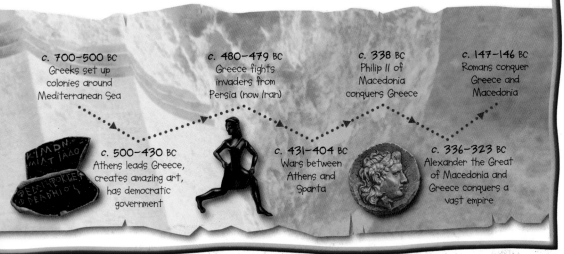

c. 700–500 BC
Greeks set up colonies around Mediterranean Sea

c. 500–430 BC
Athens leads Greece, creates amazing art, has democratic government

c. 480–479 BC
Greece fights invaders from Persia (now Iran)

c. 431–404 BC
Wars between Athens and Sparta

c. 338 BC
Philip II of Macedonia conquers Greece

c. 336–323 BC
Alexander the Great of Macedonia and Greece conquers a vast empire

c. 147–146 BC
Romans conquer Greece and Macedonia

War with Troy

54 A famous Greek poem, the Iliad, describes a terrible war between the Greeks and the Trojans. The Trojans lived in a rich city on the west coast of Asia Minor (now Turkey). The Iliad was first written down around 750 BC. Ancient Greeks said the writer was a blind poet called Homer.

▼ A scene from the 2004 film *Troy*, starring Brad Pitt. The war between the Trojans and the Greeks still thrills people today. Some of the story is legend, but it may be based on real, half-remembered, facts.

MAKE HELEN'S CROWN

You will need:
gold-coloured card   ruler   scissors   sticky tape   glue   gold plastic 'jewels' or sequins   strings of beads

1. Cut a strip of gold-coloured card about 15 cm wide and 65 cm long.

2. Stick the ends of the strip together, using tape to make a circular 'crown'.

3. Decorate your crown with 'jewels' or sequins.

4. Add strings of beads hanging down at the back and the sides.

55 Queen Helen loved a Trojan prince. According to legend, the Trojan War started because Helen, the wife of Greek King Menelaus, ran away with (or was captured by) Paris, a Trojan prince. However, historians believe the main reason for the war was because the Greeks and the Trojans were rival traders.

56 The Greeks could not break through Troy's walls until they thought of a clever plan. They made a huge, hollow, wooden horse, hid warriors inside and persuaded the Trojans to accept it as an offering to the gods. The Trojans hauled the horse into their city, then the Greeks leaped out and defeated them.

57 Odysseus survived to have amazing adventures. Another famous Greek poem tells how the warrior Odysseus fought at Troy, then on the way home survived extraordinary encounters with gods, giants, witches, one-eyed monsters, sea-serpents and a man-eating whirlpool.

▶ The Cyclops was a one-eyed giant. He trapped Odysseus and his soldiers in a cave and planned to eat them. But Odysseus blinded the Cyclops, escaped from the cave and sailed away.

▶ The Iliad describes how, for ten years, the Greeks besieged the city of Troy. They eventually won the war by offering a wooden horse to the Trojans. Once inside the city walls, warriors leapt out the horse and destroyed the city.

33

City-states

58 The power of Mycenaean kings collapsed around 1200 BC. By 700 BC, Greece had been divided into 300 city-states, which were cities and the land around them. Some city-states were ruled by kings, some by tyrants (men who governed by force) and some by oligarchs (small groups of rich, powerful men).

▶ Merchant ships carried goods from all round the Mediterranean Sea to sell in Greek markets. They could only travel in the summer, winter seas were too stormy.

59 Most city-states grew rich by buying and selling. The agora (market-place) was the centre of many cities. Goods on sale included farm produce such as grain, wine and olive oil, salt from the sea, pottery, woollen blankets, sheepskin cloaks, leather sandals and slaves.

60 Top craftsmen made fine goods for sale. Cities were home to many expert craftsmen. They ran small workshops next to their homes, or worked as slaves in factories owned by rich businessmen. Greek craftworkers were famous for producing fine pottery, stone-carvings, weapons, armour and jewellery.

61 Coins displayed city wealth and pride.

They were invented in the Near East around 600 BC. Their use soon spread to Greece, and each city state issued its own designs, stamped out of real silver. Coins were often decorated with images of gods and goddesses, heroes, monsters and favourite local animals.

▶ The design on the top coin shows the head of Alexander the Great. The other is decorated with an owl, the symbol of Athens' guardian goddess, Athena.

◀▲ The walls and gates guarding the city of Mycenae were made of huge stone slabs. The gate had a huge sculpture of two lions above it.

63 Cities were defended by strong stone walls.

City-states were proud, independent and quarrelsome. They were often at war with their rivals. They were also in constant danger of attack from neighbouring nations, especially Persia (now Iran). To protect their homes, temples, workshops, market-places and harbours, citizens built strong wooden gates and high stone walls.

62 Within most city-states, there were different classes of people.

Citizens were men who had been born in the city-state, together with their wives and children. Foreigners were traders, sailors or travelling artists and scholars. Slaves belonged to their owners.

▶ Many Greek ships were wrecked together with their cargoes. Some have survived on the seabed for over 2000 years and are studied by divers today.

Mighty Athens

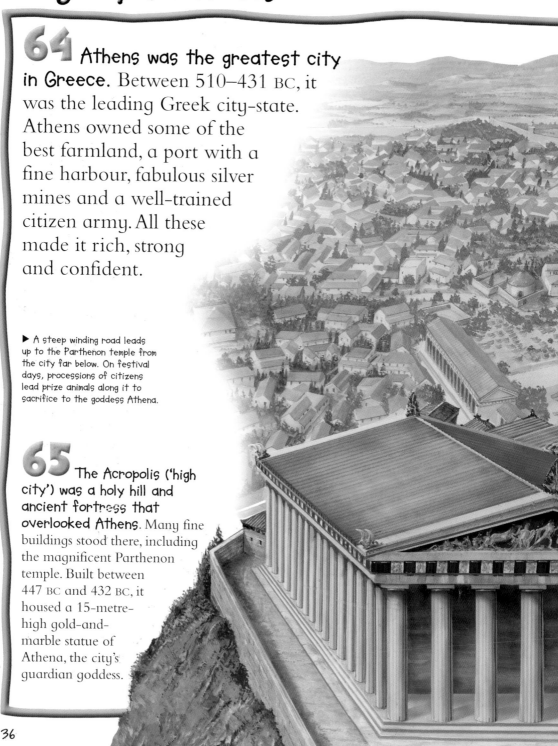

64 **Athens was the greatest city in Greece.** Between 510–431 BC, it was the leading Greek city-state. Athens owned some of the best farmland, a port with a fine harbour, fabulous silver mines and a well-trained citizen army. All these made it rich, strong and confident.

▶ A steep winding road leads up to the Parthenon temple from the city far below. On festival days, processions of citizens lead prize animals along it to sacrifice to the goddess Athena.

65 **The Acropolis ('high city') was a holy hill and ancient fortress that overlooked Athens.** Many fine buildings stood there, including the magnificent Parthenon temple. Built between 447 BC and 432 BC, it housed a 15-metre-high gold-and-marble statue of Athena, the city's guardian goddess.

66 In 490 and 480 BC, armies from Persia (now Iran) invaded Greece. They were defeated, but Greek city-states felt threatened. They joined together in a League against the Persians. Athens took charge of the League, built a splendid navy and sent soldiers and government officials to 'advise' other city-states. By around 454 BC, Athens had taken control of most of Greece.

67 Athenian city leaders paid for fine works of art. They invited the best artists, architects, sculptors, scientists and scholars to live and work in their city, and gave money to build temples, monuments and public buildings. They vowed to make their city 'an education to Greece'.

68 Athenians are famous today – after more than 2000 years! Pericles was a great general and political leader. Socrates and Plato were philosophers and teachers who taught how to think and question. Aristotle was a scientist who pioneered a new way of studying by carefully observing and recording evidence.

Sparta

69 **Sparta was Athens' great rival.** It was a city-state set in wild mountain country in the far south of Greece. Sparta had kings who ruled together with a small elite group of citizens. Other Spartans were either free craftsmen who were not allowed to vote, or helots who had few rights but made up 80 percent of the population.

70 **Sparta was always ready for war.** Kings and citizens lived in fear that the helots might rebel. So all male Spartans had to train as warriors. After this, they were sent to live in barracks with other soldiers, ready to fight at any time.

71 **All Spartan citizens were warriors.** Soldiers were famous for their bravery and loyalty – and for their bright red cloaks and long curling hair. Their main duty was to fight. They had no time to grow food, keep farm animals, build houses, make clothes or buy and sell. All these tasks, and more, were done by helot families.

I DON'T BELIEVE IT!

When their sons were marching off to war Spartan women said "Come back carrying your shield (victorious) or carried on it (dead!)".

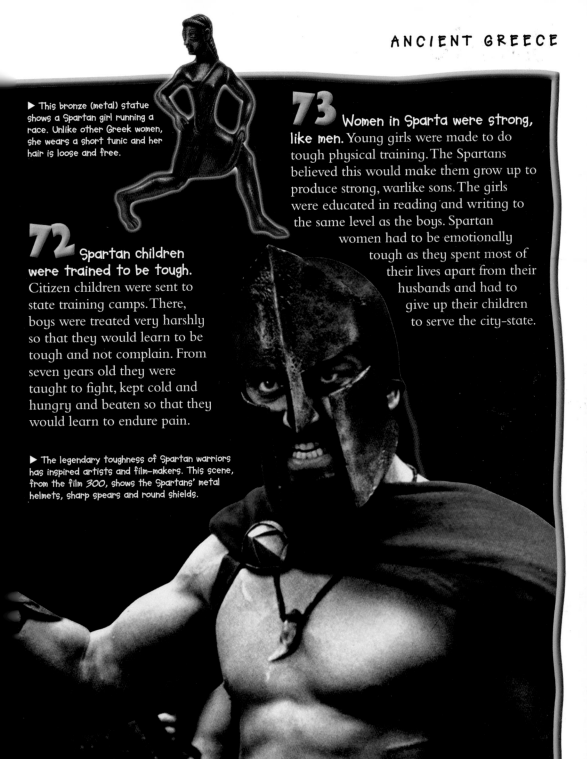

▶ This bronze (metal) statue shows a Spartan girl running a race. Unlike other Greek women, she wears a short tunic and her hair is loose and free.

73 **Women in Sparta were strong, like men.** Young girls were made to do tough physical training. The Spartans believed this would make them grow up to produce strong, warlike sons. The girls were educated in reading and writing to the same level as the boys. Spartan women had to be emotionally tough as they spent most of their lives apart from their husbands and had to give up their children to serve the city-state.

72 **Spartan children were trained to be tough.** Citizen children were sent to state training camps. There, boys were treated very harshly so that they would learn to be tough and not complain. From seven years old they were taught to fight, kept cold and hungry and beaten so that they would learn to endure pain.

▶ The legendary toughness of Spartan warriors has inspired artists and film-makers. This scene, from the film 300, shows the Spartans' metal helmets, sharp spears and round shields.

Family life

74 **Families were very important.** A person's wealth, rank and occupation all depended on their family circumstances, as did the part they played in community life. Some families were very active in politics and had powerful friends – and enemies.

76 **Fathers were the heads of families.** They had power over everyone in their households – wives, children and slaves. However, families also worked as a team to find food, make a safe, comfortable home and train their children in all the skills they would need in adult life.

Bedrooms were upstairs

Pottery tiles

Mud-brick walls covered with plaster

Slaves cooked in the kitchen

Prayers were said around the altar each morning

75 **All Greek parents longed for a son.** Boys passed on the family name to the next generation and they could protect family property and run businesses or farms. However, girls had to be fed and housed at the family's expense, then they left to get married.

▲ Greek houses were designed to provide security and privacy. They had high, windowless outer walls and a hidden inner courtyard, which only the inhabitants and trusted visitors could see.

77 **Most girls married very young, aged around 13 years.** Their husbands, who were several years older, were chosen by their fathers for political or business reasons. A marriage linked two familes together. Romantic love was not important in marriage – the Greeks thought it was dangerous!

▼ Weddings took place at dusk. The bride was driven to the bridegroom's family home, accompanied by guests carrying flaming wooden torches.

78 **Women did not have the same rights as men.** Many women had strong opinions about city and community life. A few were also well-educated and interested in the latest ideas. However, according to the law, women could not vote, make a public speech or take any part in politics.

79 **Funerals were important family occasions.** Wives and daughters spent most of their lives at home. However, they were allowed to attend family funerals. All family members said prayers together and made offerings to the gods in memory of the dead person.

Clothes and fashion

80 Greek clothes were just draped around the body. They were loose and flowing, for comfort in the hot summer months. For extra warmth in winter, both men and women draped a thick woolly himation (cloak) over their shoulders.

81 Each piece of cloth used to make a garment was specially made. It had to be the right length and width to fit the wearer. All cloth was handwoven, usually by women in their homes. Cool, smooth linen was the favourite cloth for summer. In winter, Greeks preferred cosy wool. Very rich people wore fine clothes of silk imported from India.

▶ Men's clothing was designed for action. Young men wore short tunics so they could work — and fight — easily. Older men's robes were longer.

◀ Women's clothing was modest and draped the body from top to toe. Respectable women covered their heads and faces with a veil when they went outside the house.

MAKE A GREEK CHITON

You will need:
Length of cloth twice as wide as your outstretched arms and half your height
safety pins   belt or length of cord

1. Fold the cloth in half.

2. Fasten two edges of the cloth together with safety pins, leaving a gap of about 30 cm in the middle.

3. Pull the cloth over your head so that the safety pins sit on your shoulders.

4. Fasten the belt or cord around your waist. Pull some of the cloth over the belt so that the cloth is level with your knees.

82 Women – and men – took care of their skin. To keep their skin smooth and supple, men and women rubbed themselves all over with olive oil. Rich women also used sunshades or face powder to achieve a fashionably pale complexion. They did not want to look sun-tanned – that was for farm workers, slaves – and men!

83 Curls were very fashionable. Women grew their hair long and tied it up with ribbons or headbands, leaving long curls trailing over their shoulders. Men, except for Spartan warriors, had short curly hair. Male and female slaves had their hair cropped very short – this was a shameful sign.

Before 500 BC

500–300 BC

After 300 BC

▲ Before 500 BC, long, natural hairstyles were popular. Between 500–300 BC, women tied their hair up and held it in place with ribbons or scarves. After 300 BC, curled styles and jewelled hair ornaments were popular and men shaved off their beards.

84 The Greeks liked to look good and admired fit, slim, healthy bodies. Women were praised for their grace and beauty. Young men were admired for their strong figures, and often went without clothes when training for war or taking part in sports competitions. Top athletes became celebrities, and were asked by artists to pose for them as models.

85 Sponges, showers and swimming helped the Greeks keep clean. Most houses did not have piped water. So people washed themselves by standing under waterfalls, swimming in streams or squeezing a big sponge full of water over their heads, like a shower.

◄ Athletes and their trainer (left) pictured on a Greek vase.

Gods and goddesses

86 To the Greeks, the world was full of dangers and disasters that they could not understand or control. There were also many good things, such as love, joy, music and beauty, that were wonderful but mysterious. The Greeks thought of all these unknown forces as gods and goddesses who shaped human life and ruled the world.

▶ This statue of the goddess Aphrodite was carved from white marble – a very smooth, delicate stone. It was designed to portray the goddess' perfect beauty. Sadly, it has been badly damaged over the centuries.

▶ Poseidon was god of the sea and storms. He also sent terrifying earthquakes to punish people – or cities – that offended him.

87 Gods and goddesses were pictured as superhuman creatures. They were strong and very beautiful. However, like humans, gods and goddesses also had weaknesses. Aphrodite was thoughtless, Hera was jealous, Apollo and his sister Artemis were cruel, and Ares was bad-tempered.

▲ Odysseus and his shipmates were surrounded by the Sirens – beautiful half-women, half-bird monsters. They sang sweet songs, calling sailors towards dangerous rocks where their ships were wrecked.

90 **The Greeks believed in magic spirits and monsters.** These included Gorgons who turned men to stone, and Sirens – bird-women whose song lured sailors to their doom. They also believed in witchcraft and curses and tried to fight against them. People painted magic eyes on the prows of their ships to keep a look-out for evil.

88 **Individuals were often anxious to see what the future would bring.** They believed that oracles (holy messengers) could see the future. The most famous oracles were at Delphi, where a drugged priestess answered questions, and at Dodona, where the leaves of sacred trees whispered words from the gods.

▶ Herakles was a hero – a man who became a god. He performed amazing feats of strength and fought against many monsters. This statue shows him killing a centaur, half-man, half-horse.

89 **Poets and dramatists retold myths and legends about the gods.** Some stories were explanations of natural events – thunder was the god Zeus shaking his fist in anger. Others explored bad thoughts and feelings shared by gods and humans, such as greed and disloyalty.

Olympic Games

91 **The Olympic Games began as a festival to honour Zeus.** Over the centuries, it grew into the greatest sports event in the Greek world. A huge festival complex was built at Olympia with a temple, sports tracks, seats for 40,000 spectators, a campsite and rooms for visitors and a field full of stalls selling food and drink.

▶ Victory! The Greeks believed that winners were chosen by the gods. The first known Olympic Games was held in 776 BC, though the festival may have begun years earlier.

92 **Every four years athletes travelled from all over Greece to take part in the Olympic Games.** They had to obey strict rules – respect for Zeus, no fights among competitors and no weapons anywhere near the sports tracks. In return they claimed protection – the holy Olympic Peace. Anyone who attacked them on their journeys was severely punished.

QUIZ

1. When was the first Olympic Games held?
2. Could women go to the Olympic Games?
3. What did winning athletes wear on their heads?

Answers:
1. 776 BC, though the festival may have begun years earlier 2. No. There was a separate women's games held 3. Crowns of holy laurel leaves

93 The most popular events were running, long jump, wrestling and boxing. Spectators might also watch chariot races, athletes throwing the discus and javelin or weightlifting contests. The most prestigious event was the 200-metre sprint. There was also a dangerous fighting contest called pankration (total power).

▲ Boxers did not wear gloves. Instead they wrapped their hands in bandages.

94 Many events featured weapons or skills that were needed in war. One of the most gruelling competitions was a race wearing heavy battle armour. The main Olympic Games were for men only – women could not take part. There was a separate women's games held at Olympia on different years from the men's competitions.

▲ Throwing the discus was a test of strength and balance. It was also useful training for war.

95 Athletes who won Olympic contests were honoured as heroes. They were crowned with wreaths of holy laurel leaves and given valuable prizes of olive oil, fine clothes and pottery. Poets composed songs in their praise and their home city-states often rewarded them with free food and lodgings for life!

▲ Swimmer Michael Phelps sets a new world record at the Beijing Olympics, 2008. The modern Olympics is modelled on the ancient games and since 1896 has remained the world's greatest sports festival.

▶ A crown of laurel leaves was given to winning athletes as a sign of their god-like strength and speed.

Scientists and thinkers

96 The Greeks liked to ask questions and discuss. Although they believed in gods and magic, they also wanted to investigate the world in a practical way. They learned mathematics and astronomy from the Egyptians and Babylonians then used this knowledge to find out more for themselves.

▶ Hipparchus (170–126 BC) observed and recorded the position of over 800 stars and worked out a way of measuring their brightness.

I DON'T BELIEVE IT!

Pythagoras' followers believed in reincarnation (being born again in a different body). They were vegetarians – but they would not eat beans because they might contain reborn human souls.

97 Mathematicians and astronomers made important discoveries. Aristarchus was the first to understand that the Earth travels around the Sun. Hipparchus mapped the stars. Thales discovered mathematical laws about circles and triangles. Pythagoras worked out the mathematics behind music and measured the movements of the Sun and the Moon.

98

Many people believed that illness was a punishment sent by the gods. However doctors, led by Hippocrates (460–370 BC), tried to cure people with good food, fresh air, exercise and herbal medicines. They carefully observed patients for signs of illness and recorded the results of their prescriptions. That way they could prove scientifically which treatments worked best for each disease.

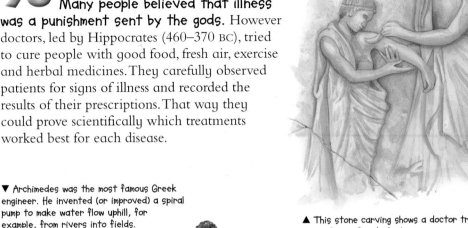

▼ Archimedes was the most famous Greek engineer. He invented (or improved) a spiral pump to make water flow uphill, for example, from rivers into fields.

▲ This stone carving shows a doctor treating an injured arm. Greek doctors were some of the first in the world to treat patients scientifically.

Handle turns wooden screw

Water is lifted round and round and then pushed out

Water is pulled in as the screw turns

99

Engineers designed many clever machines. Speakers at the Athenian Assembly were timed by a water-powered clock and there were machines that used hot air to open temple doors. Archimedes (287–211 BC) discovered how objects float and how they balance. He also designed a 'sun gun' (huge glass lens) to focus the Sun's rays on enemy ships to set them on fire.

100

Greek thinkers thought about thinking! As well as investigating the world and creating new inventions they also wanted to understand people and society. They asked questions such as 'How do we think?' 'How do we see and feel?', 'What is good?' and 'How can we live the best lives?'

The centre of an empire

101 Rome was a city in central Italy, and it ruled one of the world's greatest empires. An empire is made up of many different countries governed by a single ruler. Rome began around 1000 BC as a village of wooden huts, but soon grew rich and powerful. It was busy, crowded, noisy and exciting, with many beautiful buildings. By 200 BC the Romans ruled most of Italy, and started to invade neighbouring lands. They conquered a vast empire that stretched between what we now call Scotland and Turkey.

Capital city

102 **Over a million people lived in Rome.**
By around AD 300, Rome was the largest
city in the world. There were citizens
who could vote and serve in the army,
and there were non-citizens who did not
have these rights. The government was
run by nobles and knights who
were usually very rich. Plebeians,
or ordinary people, were
usually fairly poor but were
citizens of Rome. Slaves
were not citizens. They
were not free to leave
their owners and had
no rights.

103 The Forum was the government district in the centre of Rome.

People went there to meet their friends and business colleagues, discuss politics, and to listen to famous orators who made speeches in the open air. The Forum was mainly a market-place, surrounded by government buildings such as offices and law-courts.

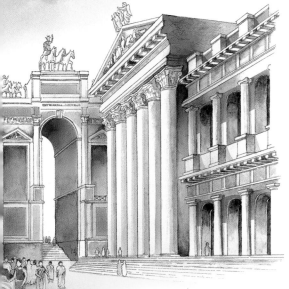

105 The Romans were great water engineers.

They designed aqueducts, raised channels to carry water from streams in far-away hills and mountains to the city. The richest Roman homes were supplied with constant running water carried in lead pipes. Ordinary people had to drink from public fountains.

106 Rome relied on its drains.

Rome was so crowded that good drains were essential. Otherwise, the citizens could have caught diseases from sewage and died. The largest sewer, called the 'cloaca maxima', was so high and so wide that a horse and cart could drive through it.

104 Rome was a well-protected city.

It was surrounded by 50 kilometres of strong stone walls, to keep out attackers. All visitors had to enter the city through one of its 37 gates, which were guarded by soldiers and watchmen.

I DON'T BELIEVE IT!

Roman engineers also designed public lavatories. These lavatories were convenient, but not private. Users sat on rows of seats, side by side!

City life

107 **The Romans built the world's first high-rise apartments.** Most of the people who lived in Ostia, a busy port close to Rome, had jobs connected with trade, such as shipbuilders and money-changers. They lived in blocks of flats known as 'insulae'. A typical block was three or four storeys high, with up to a hundred small, dirty, crowded rooms.

108 **Rich Romans had more than one home.** Rome was stuffy, dirty and smelly, especially in summer time. Wealthy Roman families liked to get away from the city to cleaner, more peaceful surroundings. They purchased a house (a 'villa urbana') just outside the city, or a big house surrounded by farmland (a 'villa rustica') in the countryside far away from Rome.

109 **Many Roman homes had a pool, but it was not used for swimming!** Pools were built for decoration, in the central courtyards of large Roman homes. They were surrounded by plants and statues. Some pools had a fountain; others had mosaics – pictures made of tiny coloured stones or squares of glass – covering the floor.

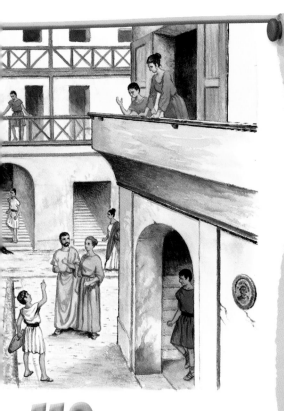

MAKE A PAPER MOSAIC

You will need:

large sheet of paper   scissors
pencil   glue
scraps of coloured and textured paper

Draw the outlines of your design on a large sheet of paper. Plan which colours to use for different parts of the mosaic.

Cut the paper scraps into small squares, all roughly the same size. The simplest way to do this is to cut strips, then snip the strips into squares.

Stick the paper squares onto the large sheet of paper following the outlines of your design.

110 Fortunate families had hot feet.

Homes belonging to wealthy families had underfloor central heating. Blasts of hot air, warmed by a wood-burning furnace, circulated in channels built beneath the floor. The furnace was kept burning by slaves who chopped wood and stoked the fire.

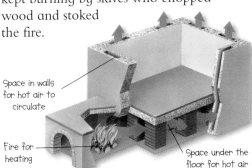

Space in walls for hot air to circulate

Fire for heating

Space under the floor for hot air

111 Rome had its own fire brigade.

The 7000 firemen were all specially trained freed slaves. Ordinary families could not afford central heating, so they warmed their rooms with fires in big clay pots which often set the house alight.

Going shopping

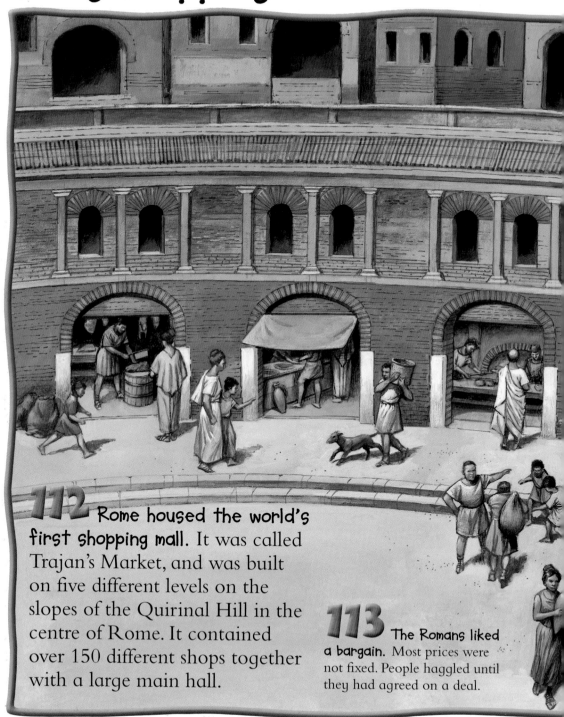

112 **Rome housed the world's first shopping mall.** It was called Trajan's Market, and was built on five different levels on the slopes of the Quirinal Hill in the centre of Rome. It contained over 150 different shops together with a large main hall.

113 **The Romans liked a bargain.** Most prices were not fixed. People haggled until they had agreed on a deal.

CAN YOU MEASURE IN ROMAN?

The Romans had different measurements to us. Find out below what they were!

A 'pes' equals 29 centimetres. If you are 1 metre 16 centimetres tall, how tall would you be in Roman measurements?

A Roman 'libra' is 326 grammes. Find out how many your favourite toy weighs?

A 'sextarius' is 450 mililitres. How many of these can you fit in a saucepan?

114 Roman shoppers had to get up early. Many shops and market-stalls closed at noon. Shoppers also had to walk a long way to make purchases as different goods were sold in different parts of the city.

Eating and drinking

115 Most Romans ate very little during the day. They had bread and water for breakfast and a light snack of bread, cheese or fruit around midday. They ate their main meal at about 4 o'clock. In rich people's homes, a meal would have three separate courses, and could last for up to three hours! Poor people ate much simpler foods, such as soups made with lentils and onions, barley porridge, peas, cabbage and tough, cheap cuts of meat stewed in vinegar.

116 Only rich Roman people had their own kitchen. They could afford to employ a chef with slaves to help him in the kitchen. Ordinary people went to 'popinae' (cheap eating houses) for their main meal, or bought ready-cooked snacks from roadside fast food stalls.

117 At parties, the Romans ate lying down. Men and women lay on long couches arranged round a table. They also often wore crowns of flowers, and took off their sandals before entering the dining room.

REAL ROMAN FOOD!

PATINA DE PIRIS (Pear Soufflé)
Ingredients:

1kg pears (peeled and cored)	a little bit of oil
	pinch of salt
	½ tsp cumin
6 eggs (beaten)	ground pepper
4 tbsp honey	to taste

Make sure that you ask an adult to help you with this recipe.
Mash the pears together with the pepper, cumin, honey, and a bit of oil. Add the beaten eggs and put into a casserole. Cook for approximately 30 minutes in a moderate oven. Serve with a little bit of pepper sprinkled on top.

◄ Dishes served at a Roman banquet might include shellfish, roast meat, eggs, vegetables, fresh fruits, pastries and honeyed wine. The Romans enjoyed strong-flavoured, spicy food, and also sweet-sour flavours.

School days

118 **Roman boys learned how to speak well.** Roman schools taught three main subjects, reading, maths – and public speaking. Boys needed all three skills for their future careers. There were no newspapers or television, so politicians, army leaders and government officials all had to make speeches in public, explaining their plans and policies to Roman crowds. Boys went to school from around seven years old and left aged 16.

▼ Roman schoolboys practise reading with their slave schoolmaster.

119 **Roman girls did not go to school.** They mostly stayed at home, where their mothers, or women slaves, taught them how to cook, clean, weave cloth and look after children. Girls from rich families, or families who ran a business, also learned to read, write and keep accounts.

▼ A girl is taught to play the lyre.

120 **Many of the best teachers were slaves.** Schoolmasters and private tutors often came from Greece. They were purchased by wealthy people who wanted to give their sons a good education. The Greeks had a long tradition of learning, which the Romans admired.

121 The Romans wrote a lot — but not on paper. They used thin slices of wood for letters and day-to-day business. For notes Romans used flat wooden boards covered with wax, as the wax could be smoothed over and used again. For important documents that they wanted to keep, the Romans used cleaned and polished calfskin, or papyrus.

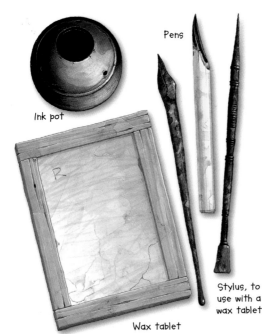

Ink pot

Pens

Stylus, to use with a wax tablet

Wax tablet

122 Romans made ink from soot. To make black ink, the Romans mixed soot from wood fires with vinegar and a sticky gum that oozed from the bark of trees. This sounds like a strange mixture, but some Roman writing has survived for almost 2000 years.

123 Rome had many libraries. Some were public, and open to everyone, others belonged to rich families and were kept shut away in their houses. It was fashionable to sponsor writers and collect their works.

124 Many Romans read standing up — it was easier that way. It took time and patience to learn how to read from a papyrus scroll. Most were at least 10 metres long. Readers held the scroll in their right hand, and a stick in their left hand. They unrolled a small section of the scroll at a time.

LEARN SOME ROMAN WORDS!

The Romans spoke a language called Latin. It forms the basis of many languages today, and below you can learn some Latin for yourself!

liber = book   epistola = letter
bibliotheca = library
vellum = calfskin
stylus = writing stick
(used with wax tablets)
librarii = slaves who work in a library
grammaticus = schoolmaster
paedagogus = private tutor

Father knows best!

125 A Roman father had the power of life and death over his family. According to Roman law, each family had to be headed by a man. He was known as the 'paterfamilias' (father of a family), and was usually the oldest surviving male. The buildings of the house and its contents belonged to him, and he had the right to punish any family members who misbehaved. Even his mother and other older female relatives were expected to obey him.

▲ The Romans gave a good luck charm, called a bulla, to their babies.

126 Roman families included more than blood relations. To the Romans, a 'family' meant all the people living and working together in the same household. So families included many different slaves and servants, as well as a husband and wife and their children.

▲ This carving shows a Roman wedding. The bride and groom are in the centre, with a priestess behind them.

127 **Sons were valued more than daughters.** The Romans preferred boys to girls. Boys would grow up to carry on the family name. They might also bring fame and honour to a family by achievements in government, politics and war. They might marry a rich wife, which helped to make the whole family richer, or win friends among powerful people.

128 **Childhood was short for a Roman girl.** Roman law allowed girls to get married at 12 years old, and many had become mothers by the time they were 15. Roman girls could not choose whom to marry, especially if they came from rich or powerful families. Instead, marriages were arranged by families, to gain political power or encourage business deals. Love was not important.

129 **Roman families liked to keep pets.** Roman statues and paintings show many children playing with their pets. Dogs, cats and doves were all popular. Some families also kept ornamental fish and tame deer.

Roman style

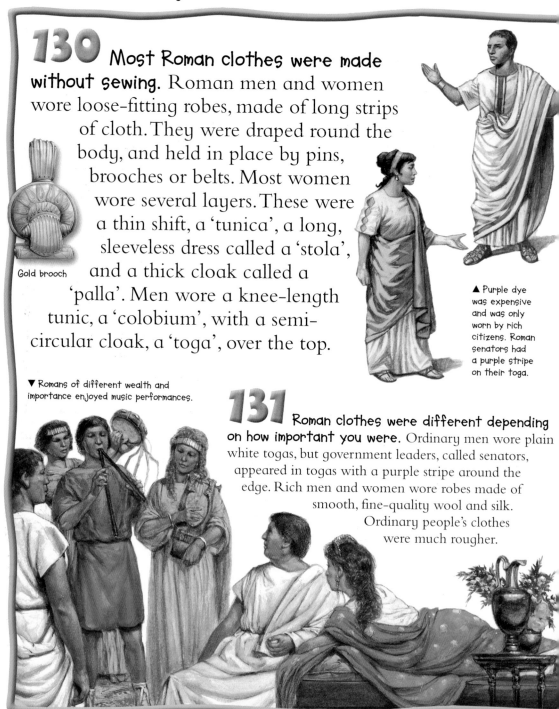

130 **Most Roman clothes were made without sewing.** Roman men and women wore loose-fitting robes, made of long strips of cloth. They were draped round the body, and held in place by pins, brooches or belts. Most women wore several layers. These were a thin shift, a 'tunica', a long, sleeveless dress called a 'stola', and a thick cloak called a 'palla'. Men wore a knee-length tunic, a 'colobium', with a semi-circular cloak, a 'toga', over the top.

Gold brooch

▲ Purple dye was expensive and was only worn by rich citizens. Roman senators had a purple stripe on their toga.

▼ Romans of different wealth and importance enjoyed music performances.

131 **Roman clothes were different depending on how important you were.** Ordinary men wore plain white togas, but government leaders, called senators, appeared in togas with a purple stripe around the edge. Rich men and women wore robes made of smooth, fine-quality wool and silk. Ordinary people's clothes were much rougher.

132 Clothes told the world who you were.

People from many different cultures and races lived in lands ruled by the Romans. They wore many different styles of clothes. For example, men from Egypt wore wigs and short linen kilts. Celtic women from northern Europe wore long woollen shawls, woven in brightly coloured checks. Celtic men wore trousers.

▼ These Roman sandals have metal studs in the soles to make sure that they don't wear down too quickly!

DRESS LIKE A ROMAN!

You can wear your very own toga! Ask an adult for a blanket or a sheet, then follow the instructions below!

 First ask an adult to find you a blanket or sheet. White is best, like the Romans.

Drape your sheet over your left shoulder. Now pass the rest behind your back.

 Pull the sheet across your front, so that you're wrapped up in it. You're almost a Roman now!

Finally, drape the last end over your right hand and there you have it, a Roman toga!

133 Roman boots were made for walking!

Roman soldiers and travellers wore lace-up boots with thick leather soles studded with iron nails. Other Roman footwear included 'socci', loose-fitting slippers to wear indoors. Farmers wore shoes made of a single piece of ox-hide wrapped round the foot, called 'carbatinae'. There were also 'crepidae', comfortable lace-up sandals with open toes.

Looking good

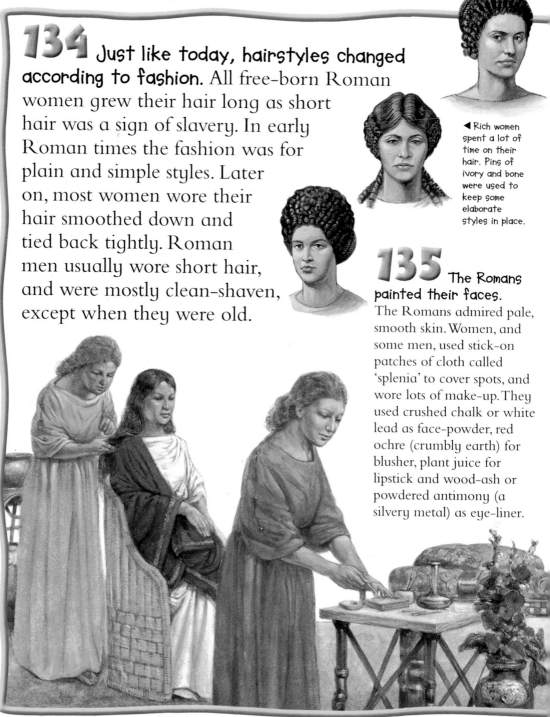

134 Just like today, hairstyles changed according to fashion. All free-born Roman women grew their hair long as short hair was a sign of slavery. In early Roman times the fashion was for plain and simple styles. Later on, most women wore their hair smoothed down and tied back tightly. Roman men usually wore short hair, and were mostly clean-shaven, except when they were old.

◄ Rich women spent a lot of time on their hair. Pins of ivory and bone were used to keep some elaborate styles in place.

135 The Romans painted their faces. The Romans admired pale, smooth skin. Women, and some men, used stick-on patches of cloth called 'splenia' to cover spots, and wore lots of make-up. They used crushed chalk or white lead as face-powder, red ochre (crumbly earth) for blusher, plant juice for lipstick and wood-ash or powdered antimony (a silvery metal) as eye-liner.

136
Blonde hair was highly prized. Most Romans were born with wiry dark brown hair. Some fashionable people admired delicate blonde hair because it was unusual. Roman women used vinegar and lye (an early form of soap, made from urine and wood-ash) to bleach their own hair.

137

Going to the barbers could be very painful. In Roman times, sharp scissors and razors had not been invented. Barbers used shears to trim men's hair and beards. When a smooth, close-shaven look was in fashion barbers had to pull men's beards out by the roots, one hair at a time!

QUIZ
If you had to dress up as a Roman, what clothes would you wear? Use the information on this and the previous page to help you draw a picture of the clothes you would need and how you might arrange your hair. Will you be a rich governor, a Celtic warrior or a soldier?

Flowers to make perfume

Olive oil

Bark used for perfume

Star anise to make perfume

Olives

Saffron for eyeshadow

Ash to darken eyelids

Perfume bottle made of onyx, a kind of black stone

138
Romans liked to smell sweet. They used olive oil (made from the crushed fruit of the olive tree) to cleanse and soften their skins, and perfumes to scent their bodies. Ingredients for perfume came from many different lands – flowers came from southern Europe, spices came from India and Africa, and sweet-smelling bark and resin came from Arabia.

139
Roman combs were made from bone, ivory or wood. Like combs today, they were designed to smooth and untangle hair, and were sometimes worn as hair ornaments. But they had another, less pleasant, purpose – they were used for combing out all the little nits and lice!

Bath time

140 **The Romans went to the public baths in order to relax.** These huge buildings were more than a place to get clean. They were also fitness centres and places to meet friends. Visitors could take part in sports, such as wrestling, do exercises, have a massage or a haircut. They could buy scented oils and perfumes, read a book, eat a snack or admire works of art in the baths own sculpture gallery!

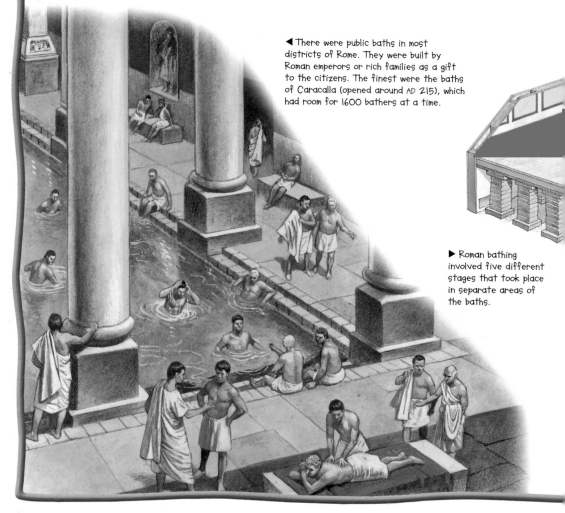

◀ There were public baths in most districts of Rome. They were built by Roman emperors or rich families as a gift to the citizens. The finest were the baths of Caracalla (opened around AD 215), which had room for 1600 bathers at a time.

▶ Roman bathing involved five different stages that took place in separate areas of the baths.

141

Men and women could not bathe together. Women usually went to the baths in the mornings, while most men were at work. Men went to the baths in the afternoons.

I DON'T BELIEVE IT!

Although the Romans liked bathing, they only visited the baths once in every nine days!

The 'frigidarium' had the coldest pool

The 'tepidarium' had a cool, or tepid, pool

The hot room was called the 'caldarium'

Fires heat the water for the hot rooms

142

Bathing wasn't simple. There were five separate stages to taking a bath Roman-style. After changing, bathers went into a very hot room, which was full of steam where they sat for a while. Then they went into a hot, dry room, where a slave removed all the sweat and dirt from their skin, using a metal scraper and olive oil. To cool off, they went for a swim in a tepid pool. Finally, they jumped into a bracing cold pool.

Having fun

143 **The Romans liked music and dancing.** Groups of buskers played in the streets, or could be hired to perform at private parties. Among ordinary families, favourite instruments included pipes, flutes, cymbals, castanets and horns. Rich, well-educated people, though, thought the noise they made was vulgar. They preferred the quieter, gentler sound of the lyre, which was played to accompany poets and singers.

▲ Roman buskers play music in the street.

Scenery could be very complicated, so it was moved around by complex machinery

Stage, or 'pulpitum'

144 **Roman theatre-goers preferred comedies to tragedies.** Comic plays had happy endings, and made audiences laugh. Tragedies were more serious, and ended with misery and suffering. The Romans also liked clowns, and invented mime, a story told without words, through gestures, acrobatic movements and dance.

145 Plays were originally part of religious festivals. Many famous dramas showed scenes from ancient myths and legends, and were designed to make people think about morals and politics. Later, plays were written on all sorts of topics – including politics and current affairs. Some were paid for by rich politicians, to spread their political message. They handed out free tickets to Roman citizens, hoping to win votes.

◄ All the parts in Roman plays were performed by men. For women's roles, men wore masks and dressed in female costume. Women could not be actors, except in mime.

146 Theatres were huge well-built structures. One of the best preserved Roman theatres is at Orange, in southern France. It has seats for almost 10,000 people. It is so cleverly designed, that the audience can hear the actors even from the back row.

147 Roman actors all wore masks. Masks helped the audience in big theatres see what each character was feeling. They were carved and painted in bright colours, with larger than life features and exaggerated expressions. Some masks were happy, some were frightened, some were sad.

148 Other favourite pastimes included games of skill and chance. Roman adults and children enjoyed dice and knucklebones, which needed nimble fingers, and draughts which relied on luck and quick thinking. They played these for fun, but adults also made bets on who would win.

I DON'T BELIEVE IT!

Roman actors were almost all men. Some were as popular as TV stars today. Women couldn't sit near the stage, in case they tried to arrange a date with one of the stars!

Let the games begin!

149 Romans admired gladiators for their strength, bravery and skill. However, gladiators' lives were short and their deaths were horrible. They were sent to the arena to fight – and suffer – until they died.

Large fork, called a trident

Net to trap opponent

Gladius, a gladiator's sword

Greaves to protect the legs

150 Most gladiators did not choose to fight. They were either prisoners-of-war or criminals who were sold to fight-trainers who organized gladiator shows. Some were specially trained, so that they would survive for longer and provide better entertainment for the watching crowds.

151 Gladiators fought wild beasts, as well as each other. Fierce wild animals were brought from distant parts of the Roman empire to be killed by gladiators in the arenas in Rome. So many lions were taken from North Africa that they became extinct there.

152 The Colosseum was an amazing building for its time. Also known as the Flavian Amphitheatre, the Colosseum was a huge oval arena in the centre of Rome, used for gladiator fights and mock sea-battles. It opened in AD 80, and could seat 50,000 people. It was built of stone, concrete and marble and had 80 separate entrances. Outside, it was decorated with statues of famous Roman heroes.

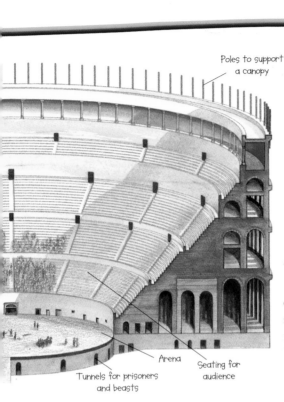

Poles to support
a canopy

Arena   Seating for
            audience

Tunnels for prisoners
and beasts

▲ The Colosseum was the largest
amphitheatre in the Roman empire.

154 Chariots often collided and overturned.

Each charioteer carried a sharp knife, called a 'falx', to cut himself free from the wreckage. Even so, many horses and charioteers were killed.

153 Some Romans preferred a day at the races.

Horses pulled fast chariots round race-tracks, called 'circuses'. The most famous was the Circus Maximus in Rome, which had room for 250,000 spectators. There could be up to 24 races each day. Twelve chariots took part in each race, running seven times round the oval track – a total distance of about 8 kilometres.

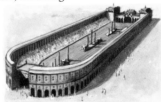

The Circus Maximus

I DON'T BELIEVE IT!

Some gladiators became so popular that people used to write graffiti about them on the walls of buildings around Rome!

155 Racing rivalries sometimes led to riots.

Races were organized by four separate teams – the Reds, Blues, Greens and Whites. Charioteers wore tunics in their teams' colours. Each team had a keen – and violent – group of fans.

Ruling Rome

156
Rome used to be ruled by kings. According to legend, the first king was Romulus, who came to power in 753 BC. Six more kings ruled after him, but they were unjust and cruel. The last king, Tarquin the Proud, was overthrown in 509 BC. After that, Rome became a republic, a state without a king. Every year the people chose two senior lawyers called consuls to head the government. Many other officials were elected, or chosen by the people, too. The republic lasted for over 400 years.

▲ Roman coin showing the emperor Constantine.

▼ Senators were men from leading citizen families who had served the Roman republic as judges or state officials. They made new laws and discussed government plans.

157
In 47 BC a successful general called Julius Caesar declared himself dictator. This meant that he wanted to rule on his own for life. Many people feared that he was trying to end the republic, and rule like the old kings. Caesar was murdered in 44 BC by a group of his political enemies. After this, there were many years of civil war.

Julius Caesar

158
In 27 BC an army general called Octavian seized power in Rome. He declared himself 'First Citizen', and said he would bring back peace and good government to Rome. He ended the civil war, and introduced many strong new laws. But he also changed the Roman government for ever. He took a new name, 'Augustus' and became the first emperor of Rome.

Octavian

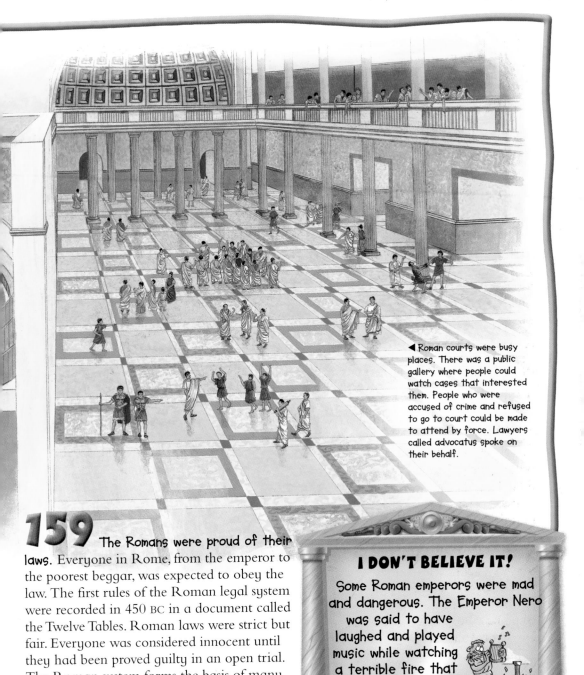

◄ Roman courts were busy places. There was a public gallery where people could watch cases that interested them. People who were accused of crime and refused to go to court could be made to attend by force. Lawyers called advocatus spoke on their behalf.

159 The Romans were proud of their laws. Everyone in Rome, from the emperor to the poorest beggar, was expected to obey the law. The first rules of the Roman legal system were recorded in 450 BC in a document called the Twelve Tables. Roman laws were strict but fair. Everyone was considered innocent until they had been proved guilty in an open trial. The Roman system forms the basis of many legal systems today.

I DON'T BELIEVE IT!

Some Roman emperors were mad and dangerous. The Emperor Nero was said to have laughed and played music while watching a terrible fire that destroyed a large part of Rome.

In the army

160 **Being a soldier was a good career, if you did not get killed!** Roman soldiers were well paid and well cared for. The empire needed troops to defend its land against enemy attack. A man who fought in the Roman army received a thorough training in battle skills. If he showed promise, he might be promoted and receive extra pay. When he retired after 20 or 25 years of service, he was given money or land to help him start a business.

161 **The Roman army contained citizens and 'helpers'.** Roman citizens joined the regular army, which was organized into legions of around 5000 men. Men who were not citizens could also fight for Rome. They were known as auxiliaries, or helpers, and were organized in special legions of their own.

162 **Roman troops carried three main weapons.** They fought with javelins, swords and daggers. Each man had to buy his own set. He looked after them carefully – one day, his life might depend on them.

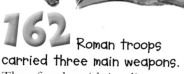

▶ Soldiers used their shields to make a protective shell. It was called a 'testudo', or tortoise.

▼ Roman troops defended the empire from attack, they were well paid but it was a dangerous job.

164 **The army advanced 30 kilometres every day.** When they were hurrying to put down a rebellion, or moving from fort to fort, Roman soldiers travelled quickly, on foot. Troops marched along straight, well-made army roads. On the march, each soldier had to carry a heavy pack. It contained weapons, armour, tools for building a camp, cooking pots, dried food and spare clothes.

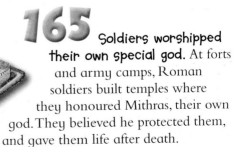

163 **Soldiers needed many skills.** In enemy territory, soldiers had to find or make everything they needed to survive. When they first arrived they built camps of tents, but soon afterwards they built permanent forts defended by strong walls. Each legion contained men with a wide range of skills, such as cooks, builders, carpenters, doctors, blacksmiths and engineers – but they all had to fight!

165 **Soldiers worshipped their own special god.** At forts and army camps, Roman soldiers built temples where they honoured Mithras, their own god. They believed he protected them, and gave them life after death.

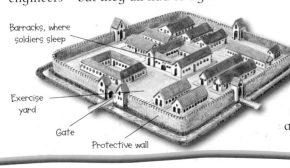

Barracks, where soldiers sleep

Exercise yard

Gate

Protective wall

Ruled by Rome

166 **More than 50 million people were ruled by Rome.** Celts, Germans, Iberians, Dacians and many other peoples lived in territory conquered by Roman armies. They spoke many different languages, and had different customs and beliefs. Roman rulers sent armies to occupy their lands, and governors to rule them. They forced conquered peoples to pay Roman taxes and obey Roman laws.

▲ A Roman tax collector assesses a farmer for taxes.

▼ Boudica, Queen of the Iceni tribe, led a revolt against the Romans.

167 **A few conquered kings and queens refused to accept Roman rule.** For example, in AD 60 Boudicca, queen of the Iceni tribe who lived in eastern England, led a rebellion against the Romans in Britain. Her army marched on the city of London and set fire to it, before being defeated by Roman soldiers. Boudicca survived the battle, but killed herself by taking poison so that she would not be captured by Roman troops.

168 **Cleopatra used beauty and charm to stop the Romans invading.** Cleopatra was queen of Egypt, in North Africa. Cleopatra knew that the Egyptian army would not be able to defeat Roman soldiers. Two Roman army generals, Julius Caesar and Mark Antony, fell in love with her. She stopped the Romans invading for many years, but Egypt was eventually conquered.

Cleopatra

▼ A carving from Trajan's column of Roman legionaries boarding ships.

169 **Roman conquerors built monuments to celebrate their victories.** Trajan, who ruled from AD 98–117, was a famous soldier who became emperor of Rome. He led Roman armies on one of their most successful conquests, in Dacia (Romania) in AD 106. To record this achievement, he gave orders for a tall stone pillar (now known as Trajan's Column) to be built in the Forum in Rome. It was almost 30 metres high, and was decorated with carvings of 2500 Roman soldiers winning wars.

Trajan's column

▲ A carving from Trajan's column of Roman soldiers building the walls of a new fort.

The farming life

170 **Rome relied on farmers.**
Most people in Roman times
lived in the countryside and
worked on farms. Farmers
produced food for city-dwellers.
Without them, the citizens would
not have survived. Food was
grown on big estates by teams
of slaves, and on small peasant
farms where single families
worked together.

171 **Farm produce was imported from
all over the empire.** Wool and honey came
from Britain, wine came from Greece,
and 400,000 tonnes of wheat were
shipped across the Mediterranean
Sea from Egypt every year. It
was ground into flour, which
was used to make
bread, the Romans'
staple, or basic, food.

172 **Farmers had no big machines
to help them.** Heavy work was done by
animals, or by human muscle-power. Ploughs
were pulled by oxen. Ripe crops were
harvested by men and women with curved
knives called sickles, and loaded by hand onto
farm carts. Donkeys turned mill wheels to
crush olives and grind grain, and to raise
drinking water from wells.

Beehives
for honey

Treading grapes
for wine

Owner of
the farm

▲ A large Roman farm estate
with slaves working the land.

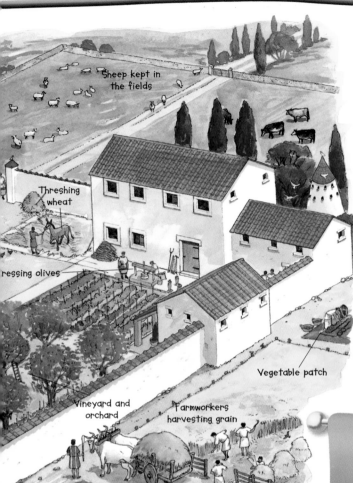

Sheep kept in the fields

Threshing wheat

ressing olives

Vegetable patch

Vineyard and orchard

Farmworkers harvesting grain

174 The most valuable fruit was small, hard, green and bitter! It came from olive trees. Olives could be pickled in salty water to eat with bread and cheese, or crushed to provide oil. The Romans used olive oil as a medicine, for cooking and preserving food, for cleaning and softening the skin, and even for burning in lamps.

173 Roman grapes grew on trees! Vines, climbing plants that produce grapes, were planted among fruit trees in Roman orchards. They provided support for the vine stems, and welcome shade to stop the grapes getting scorched by the sun. Grapes were one of the most important crops on Roman farms. The ripe fruits were picked and dried to become raisins, or pulped and made into wine.

QUIZ

Imagine that you are a Roman farmer, talking to a visitor from the city. How would you answer their questions:

What crops do you grow?
Why do you keep oxen?
Who will harvest that grain?
How do you grind grain into flour?
Why are you growing olives?

Work like a slave!

175 Roman people were not all equal.
There were different classes within Roman
society. Throughout the Roman Empire, the
biggest difference between people was
whether they were slaves or free. Free-born
men and women had rights that were
guaranteed by law, for example, to find
their own work, or travel from one place
to another. In Rome, citizens also had the
right to vote for government officials,
and to receive free hand-outs of food.
But slaves had hardly any rights at all.
They belonged to their owners just like
dogs or horses.

176 Slaves were trained to do all
sorts of tasks. Slaves did everything their
owners demanded, from babycare to hard labour
on farms. Many slaves were trusted by their
owners, who valued their skills. A few slaves
became respected chefs or doctors.

▶ Slaves were bought and sold at slave-markets like
this one. They were paraded before the citizens to
be chosen or rejected. The slaves could not
leave, or choose what work to do. They
could be cruelly punished, neglected or
given away.

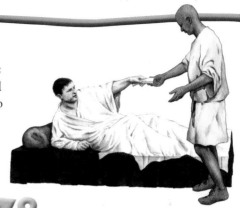

177

There were many different ways of becoming a slave. Slaves might be captured in war, purchased from a slave-trader or born to slave parents. They could also be people condemned to slavery as punishment for a serious crime.

178

Slaves were sometimes set free by their owners. Freedom could be a reward for loyalty or long service. Some sick or dying slave-owners gave orders that their slaves should be freed. They did not want their slaves to pass to a new owner who might treat them badly.

I DON'T BELIEVE IT!

From 73 BC to 71 BC a slave called Spartacus led a revolt in southern Italy. He ran away to a hideout in the hills where 90,000 other slaves joined him.

179

Some slaves did very well after they were freed. Former slaves used the skills they had learned to set up businesses of their own. Many were successful, and a few became very rich.

Roman know-how

180 **The Romans pioneered many new building materials and designs.** They discovered concrete, which was much cheaper and easier to use than solid building stone. They made bricks of clay baked at high temperatures, which lasted much longer than unbaked ones. They found out how to use arches to create tall, strong walls and doorways. They designed massive domes for buildings that were too big to be roofed with wooden beams.

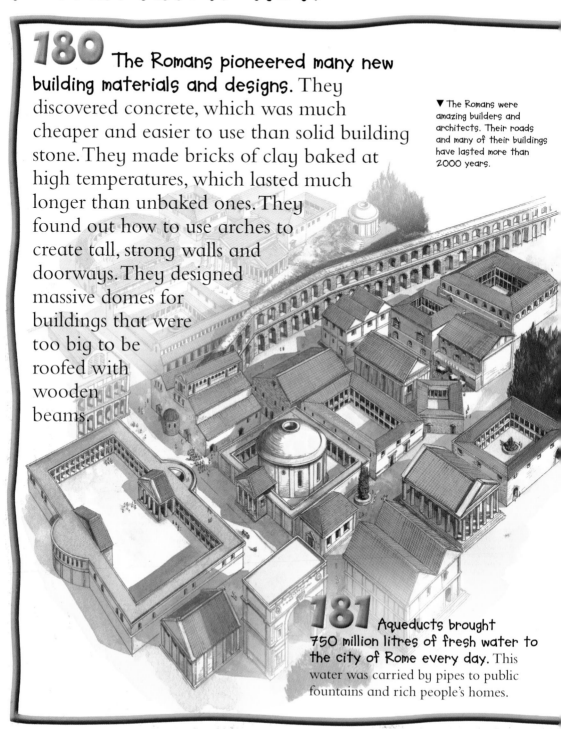

▼ The Romans were amazing builders and architects. Their roads and many of their buildings have lasted more than 2000 years.

181 **Aqueducts brought 750 million litres of fresh water to the city of Rome every day.** This water was carried by pipes to public fountains and rich people's homes.

◀ ▲ This is a Roman valve that allowed water to be pumped uphill. Water would then come out of fountains such as the one shown here.

182 **The Roman's water supplies were so advanced that no one had anything better until the 1800s!** They invented pumps with valves to pump water uphill. This went into high tanks above fountains. Gravity pulled the water out of the fountain's spout.

184 **Even the best doctors often failed to cure their patients.** But Roman doctors were skilled at sewing up cuts and joining broken bones. They also used herbs for medicines and painkillers.

▼ Romans believed in the ability of doctors to cure illnesses, but also thought witchcraft was the cause of ill health.

183 **Despite their advanced technology, Romans believed that illness was caused by witchcraft.** To find a cure, they gave presents to the witch, begging her to remove the spell, or made a special visit to a temple, to ask the gods to make them better.

Prayers and sacrifices

185 **The Romans worshipped many different gods.** Jupiter, the king of the gods, protected Roman lands. His wife Juno was worshipped by married women. Mars was the god of war, Venus was the goddess of love. Diana, the moon goddess, guarded young girls and wild animals; Neptune, god of the sea, sent earthquakes and terrible storms. Vesta was the goddess of Roman homes. Her priestesses tended a holy flame in a temple in the Forum in Rome.

Jupiter, king of the gods Juno, queen of the gods

Mercury, t messenger the gods

Neptune, god of the sea

Mars, god of war

Minerva, goddess of war

Venus, goddess of love

Diana, goddess of the moon and hunting

Pan, god of the mountainside, pastures, sheep and goats

Dis (Pluto), god of the underworld

186 **The Roman emperor was also chief priest.** As part of his government duties he said prayers and offered sacrifices to the gods who protected Rome. He was given a special name 'pontifex maximus', which meant chief bridge-builder, because people believed he acted as a bridge between the gods and ordinary people.

187 Families made
offerings to the gods every day.
They left food, wine and incense in
front of a shrine in their house. A shrine
is like a mini temple. It contained
statues of ancient gods called the 'lares'
and 'penates'. The lares were ancestor
spirits, who looked after living family
members. The penates guarded the
family's food.

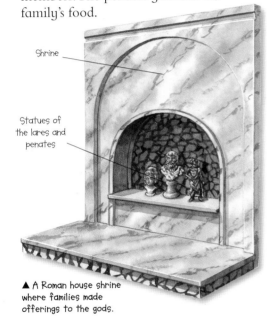

Shrine

Statues of
the lares and
penates

▲ A Roman house shrine
where families made
offerings to the gods.

188 Roman people were very
superstitious. They decorated their homes
with magic symbols, and hung good luck
charms round children's necks. They believed
that they could foretell the future by
observing animals, birds, insects and even the
weather! For example, bees were a sign of
riches and happiness but a hooting owl
foretold danger.

189 Roman men and
women could ask the gods to
curse their enemies. They
wrote their enemies' names, plus
curse words, on metal or pottery scraps
and left them at temples. They hoped that
the gods would see them and harm the
people they named in them.

▲ A Christian in Roman times praying in a catacomb.

190 Some of the world's first
Christians lived in Rome. But until
AD 313 Christianity was banned in the
Roman Empire. Christians met secretly, in
underground passages called catacombs,
to say prayers and hold services. They
also used the catacombs as a burial place.

I DON'T BELIEVE IT!

After an animal had been
sacrificed to the gods, a priest,
called a 'haruspex', examined
its liver. If it
was diseased,
bad luck was
on the way!

On the move

191 All roads led to Rome. The city was at the hub of a network of roads that stretched for more than 85,000 kilometres. They had been built to link outlying parts of the empire to the capital, so that Roman armies or government officials could travel quickly. To make travel as quick as possible, roads were built in straight lines, taking the shortest route.

▲ This map shows the Roman Empire in brown, and the roads that they built in black.

192 Rome's first main road was built in 312 BC. Its name was the Via Appia ('via' is the Latin word for road), and it ran from the city of Rome to the port of Brundisium on the south-east coast of Italy. Many travellers from Greece arrived there, and the new road made their journey to Rome quicker and easier.

193 Some Roman roads have survived for over 2000 years! Each road was made of layers of earth and stones on top of a firm, flat foundation. It was surfaced with stone slabs or gravel. The centre had a camber, a curved surface, so that rainwater drained away into ditches on either side.

Large surface slabs

Drainage ditch

Route accurately marked out

Solid foundations

194
Roman engineers used tools to help them to make accurate surveys. They made careful plans and took measurements before starting any big building project, such as a new road or city walls.

▲ These road builders are using a 'groma' to measure straight lines.

195
Poor people had to walk everywhere. They could not afford to hire a horse or a donkey, or a cushioned carriage, pulled by oxen. If they were lucky, they might manage to hitch a lift in a lumbering farm wagon – but this would not give them a comfortable ride!

196
Town streets were crowded and very dirty. Rich people travelled in curtained beds called litters, carried shoulder-high by slaves. Ordinary people used stepping-stones to avoid the mud and rubbish underfoot.

197
Heavy loads often travelled by water. There were no big lorries in Roman times! Ships powered by sails and by slaves rowing carried people and cargo across the sea and along rivers. But water-transport was slow, and could be dangerous. Roman ships were often attacked by pirates, and shipwrecks were common.

▲ The Romans' knowledge of ship-building came from the Greeks. The Romans, though, were not really sailors, and they did not improve the designs.

89

Digging up Rome

198 **Large amounts of evidence survives to tell us about Roman times.** Archaeologists have discovered the remains of many Roman buildings throughout Roman empire lands, including palaces, forts, walls, aqueducts, temples, hospitals, theatres and ordinary family homes. They have also found Roman works of art, together with glittering gold and silver coins, beautiful jewellery, fine pottery and delicate glass, and many tools and household objects used by Roman men and women in their daily lives.

Intricate Roman mosaic

These are lamps that burned olive oil for light

Statues can give us an idea what the Romans looked like

199 **We can still see many Roman designs today.** Until the 20th century, grand, important buildings were often planned and decorated in Roman style. Architects believed that Roman designs inspired respect in anyone who saw them. For this reason, many big cities in Europe, America and elsewhere have churches, museums, art-galleries, colleges and even banks that look like Roman temples or Roman villas.

Roman pots

QUIZ

1. Who was the king of the Roman gods?
2. What is the proper name for a mini temple in someone's house?
3. When was Rome's first road built?
4. What is the proper name for a curtained bed?

Answers:
1. Jupiter 2. A shrine 3. 312 BC 4. A litter

Roman coins show the most important people of the time, often the emperor

Roman people liked intricate and expensive jewellery

▲ An archaeologist's dig uncovers remains from the Roman period. Their finds give us a better understanding of how the Romans lived.

200 Many people still have Roman names. In many parts of the world, parents still like to give their children Roman names, or names based on Latin words. Here are some popular ones: Amanda (Loveable), Diana (Moon Goddess), Venus (Goddess of Love), Patricia (Noble), Laura (Laurel-tree), Virginia (Maiden), Julius (Roman family name), Antony (Roman family name), Martin (God of War), Marcus (God of War), Victor (Winner), Vincent (Conqueror).

The great games

201 **Gladiators were made to fight to the death to please the crowd.** They fought in an arena (open space surrounded by tiered seats) and used lots of different swords, spears, knives and other weapons. Not every gladiatorial fight ended in death. Some gladiators were allowed to live if they fought bravely and with skill. Most fights took place in Rome, but cities throughout the Roman Empire had arenas for these events. The arenas were also used for wild animal hunts and for the execution of criminals. For the ancient Romans, violence and bloodshed were used as entertainment.

▶ A defeated gladiator appeals for mercy from the crowd by raising his left hand. The victorious fighter awaits the instruction to kill or spare his rival.

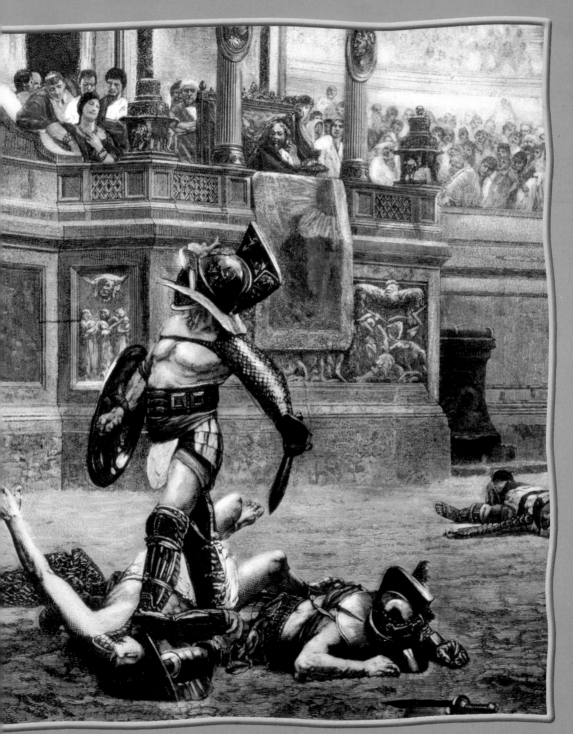

The first gladiators

202 **The first gladiators were not from Rome.** The Romans did not invent the idea of gladiators. They believed the idea of men fighting in an arena probably came to Rome from the region of Etruria. But the first proper gladiators probably came from Campania, an area of Italy south of Rome.

▲ The city of Rome began as a small town between Etruria and Campania in central Italy.

203 **The first Roman gladiators fought in 264 BC.** Six slaves were set to fight each other with swords, but they were not allowed to wear any armour. The fights did not last long before one of the slaves in each pair was killed.

▶ The gladius was the standard weapon used by early gladiators.

204 The first
gladiatorial fights were always
part of a funeral. The name
for a gladiatorial show, a munus,
means a duty owed to the dead.
The first fights were held at the
funerals of politicians and
noblemen, who ordered the
games in their wills.

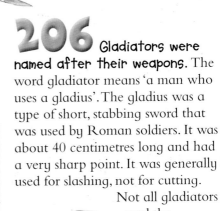

▶ The first gladiators
were usually elderly
slaves or troublemakers,
who would not be missed
much by their owners.

205 In early funeral games,
food was more important than
gladiators. The Romans used
funerals to show off how wealthy and
important they were. Free food and
drink were laid out at the funeral
for any Roman citizen who
wanted to come along. Gifts
of money, jewellery and
clothing were also handed out.
The family of the person being buried would
wear their finest clothes. The first gladiator fights
were just one part of the whole funeral.

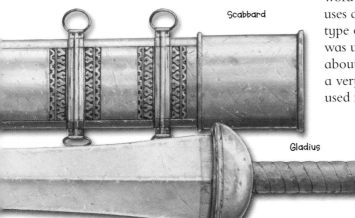

Scabbard

Gladius

206 Gladiators were
named after their weapons. The
word gladiator means 'a man who
uses a gladius'. The gladius was a
type of short, stabbing sword that
was used by Roman soldiers. It was
about 40 centimetres long and had
a very sharp point. It was generally
used for slashing, not for cutting.
Not all gladiators
used the
gladius, but the
name was used
for all fighters
in the arena.

Prisoners of war

▼ A Thracian armed with a square shield and curved sword faces a Samnite equipped with a larger shield and longer, straight sword.

Samnite

Thracian

207 **Prisoners of war fought in the arena.** Between 250 BC and 100 BC the Romans fought many wars against foreign enemies. Prisoners captured in these wars were sold as slaves in Rome. Captured soldiers were made to fight in the arena, with weapons and armour from their own country.

208 **The Samnites had the best weapons.** The Romans fought a long series of wars against the Samnites between 343 BC and 290 BC. These men each carried a large, oval shield and wore a helmet with cheek guards (flaps that protected their cheeks). Samnite gladiators were famous for the quality of their swords and spears.

209 **The Thracians had the strangest weapons.** The men from the kingdom of Thrace carried small shields and wore helmets with crests. They were famous for being able to hit any target with their spears and carried short, curved swords. This mix of weapons proved very popular and many gladiators adopted them. They became known as Thracian gladiators, even if they were not from Thrace.

I DON'T BELIEVE IT!

At the end of a war the prisoners were auctioned as slaves in the Forum (market square). Sometimes so many prisoners had been taken that the auction lasted for many days.

▶ The tall, fair-skinned Celts decorated their bodies and shields with bright colours.

210 **Celts painted their bodies before going into battle.** The Celts were the only people to have captured Rome, in 390 BC. They lived in northern Italy and across Europe. The Romans forced many Celtic prisoners to fight in their native clothes and with native weapons.

◀ The Numidians from North Africa were famous for their skill on horseback. They often fought in the arena using light javelins.

211 **The Numidians fought on horseback.** Numidia was an area of northern Africa in what is now Algeria. The area was famous for breeding quality horses and its army included large numbers of cavalry (soldiers on horseback). Prisoners of war from Numidia rode horses when they appeared in the arena.

Gladiators and politics

▲ A person's ashes were stored in a pot or urn until the funeral.

212 **Funerals were delayed for years.** Gladiatorial shows were organized as part of the funerals of rich and powerful noblemen. However, the heir of the man who had died would want to hold the show when he was standing for election so that he could impress the voters.

213 **A good gladiator show could win an election.** In ancient Rome, votes were not cast in secret. Each voter had to give his name to an official called a censor and then declare how he was voting. The men standing for election stood near the censor to see how people voted. Putting on an impressive gladiator show could gain votes.

▼ A citizen waiting to vote at an election. The censor kept a list of everyone entitled to vote and people had to prove who they were before voting.

I DON'T BELIEVE IT!

In 165 BC, a play was interrupted when the entire audience left the theatre to watch a gladiatorial show. All the actors were left alone in the theatre!

214
Some politicians hired gangs of gladiators to beat up their opponents. If a citizen could not be persuaded, by gladiator shows or the payment of money, to vote for a certain candidate, the candidate might use gladiators to bully him. Gladiators were armed with clubs and given the names of citizens who should be threatened. Every election was accompanied by this sort of violence.

▲ Men were posted at the entrance to the arena to ensure that only voters entered.

215
The best seats went to men who donated money to the election campaign. Standing for an election cost a lot of money in ancient Rome. Rich men would give or lend money to the candidate they preferred. In return they would get the best seats in a gladiatorial show and would expect to receive titles or government money if their candidate won.

216
Only voters could watch the games. The purpose of holding spectacular gladiatorial shows was to influence voters. Only citizens of Rome could vote, so only they were allowed to attend the shows. Citizens who were known to be voting for an opponent were turned away, as were slaves and foreigners who could not vote.

◀ Roman coins were made of gold, silver or bronze and carried a portrait of the emperor on one side.

Spartacus!

217 The most famous gladiator of all was Spartacus. He led a rebellion of gladiators and other slaves in the year 73BC. At first Spartacus had just 70 gladiators with him, but later over 40,000 runaway slaves joined his forces.

218 **Spartacus was a gladiator from the kingdom of Thrace.** He joined the Roman army, but did not like it and tried to run away. As a punishment, Spartacus was sent to train as a gladiator, although he was allowed to take his wife with him.

219 **The gladiators, led by Spartacus, defeated the Roman army.** After breaking out of the gladiator school (called a ludus), Spartacus hid on the slopes of Mount Vesuvius, near Naples. He defeated a small Roman force sent to capture him and then led his growing army to northern Italy. There, at Modena, he defeated a large Roman army and stole valuable goods.

220 **Spartacus wanted to cross the Alps, a large mountain range.** After winning the battle at Modena, Spartacus wanted to return to Thrace. However, his men wanted to raid cities. They made Spartacus lead them back to southern Italy.

221 **The wrong general was credited for defeating Spartacus.** Spartacus and his army of slaves and gladiators were defeated by a new Roman army at Lucania. This army was commanded by Marcus Licinius Crassus. One small group of slaves fled the battle and was captured by a commander named Gnaeus Pompey. He then rode to Rome and announced that he had defeated the rebels.

◀ The 1960 movie *Spartacus* starred Kirk Douglas (centre) as the escaped gladiator. Spartacus equipped his army of gladiators and slaves with weapons stolen from the Romans.

Caesar's games

222 **Julius Caesar borrowed money to buy his gladiators.** Julius Caesar rose to become the ruler of the Roman Empire. Early in his career he staged spectacular games to win votes in elections. But Caesar was too poor to afford to pay the bills, so he borrowed money from richer men. When he won the elections, Caesar repaid the men with favours and titles.

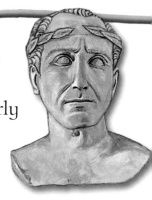

▲ Julius Caesar (102–44 BC) was a politician who won several elections after staging magnificent games to entertain the voters.

223 Caesar's gladiators fought in silver armour. In 65 BC, Julius Caesar staged the funeral games for his father, who had died 20 years earlier. Caesar was standing for election to be chief priest of Rome. To make his games even more special, Caesar dressed his 640 gladiators in armour made of solid silver.

▲ War elephants were popular attractions, and gladiators were specially trained in how to fight against them.

224 Caesar brought war elephants to Rome. In 46 BC Julius Caesar celebrated a victory in North Africa by staging gladiatorial games in Rome. Among the prisoners of war forced to fight in the arena were 40 war elephants, together with the men trained to fight them.

225

Caesar turned senators (governors of Rome) into gladiators. On one occasion Caesar forced two rich noblemen to fight in the arena. They had been sentenced to death by a court, but Caesar ordered that the man who killed the other in the arena could go free.

226

Caesar's final show was too big for the arena. The games staged by Julius Caesar when he wanted to become dictator of Rome were the grandest ever held. After weeks of shows and feasts, the final day saw a fight between two armies of 500 infantry (foot soldiers) and 30 cavalry. The battle was so large it had to be held in the enormous chariot race course, Circus Maximus.

QUIZ

1. Did Caesar's gladiators wear armour made of silver, gold or bronze?
2. Was Caesar's final show a big or small show?
3. Where did Caesar get the money to buy gladiators?

Answers:
1. Silver. 2. It was a big show.
3. He borrowed money from richer men.

▼ Chariot racing was a hugely popular sport that thrilled the crowds in ancient Rome.

The mob

227 **The Roman mob could overpower emperors.** Over a million people lived in ancient Rome. Many were voting citizens who did not have regular jobs. Even the most powerful emperors had to keep this vast mob of Romans happy. If an emperor did not put on impressive gladiatorial shows he could be booed, attacked or even be killed.

▲ Emperor Vitellius (AD 69) was murdered by a mob of Romans after failing to put on any impressive games.

▼ The seats in the arena were numbered and cushions were sometimes provided for extra comfort.

228 **Each seat was saved for a particular person.** People attending the gladiator games had their own seats. The row and seat number were written on small clay tablets that were handed out by the organizer of the games. Some seats were given to whoever queued up outside the arena.

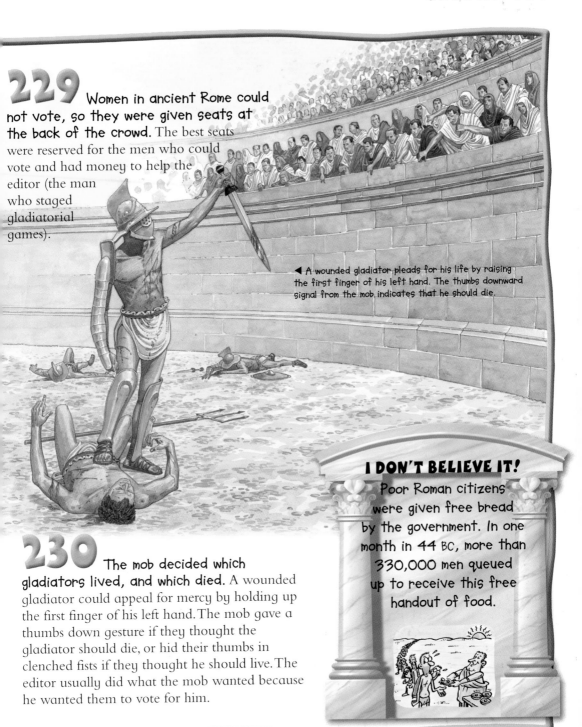

229 Women in ancient Rome could not vote, so they were given seats at the back of the crowd. The best seats were reserved for the men who could vote and had money to help the editor (the man who staged gladiatorial games).

◄ A wounded gladiator pleads for his life by raising the first finger of his left hand. The thumbs downward signal from the mob indicates that he should die.

230 The mob decided which gladiators lived, and which died. A wounded gladiator could appeal for mercy by holding up the first finger of his left hand. The mob gave a thumbs down gesture if they thought the gladiator should die, or hid their thumbs in clenched fists if they thought he should live. The editor usually did what the mob wanted because he wanted them to vote for him.

I DON'T BELIEVE IT!
Poor Roman citizens were given free bread by the government. In one month in 44 BC, more than 330,000 men queued up to receive this free handout of food.

105

Amazing arenas

231 The first gladiator fights took place in the cattle market. The cattle market, or Forum Boarium, was a large open space by the river Tiber. Cattle pens were cleared away to make space for fighting, while the audience watched from shops and temples.

◄ The crowd watched early gladiatorial fights in the cattle market from shops and pavements.

232 Most fights took place in the Forum. This was the largest open square in the centre of Rome. The most important temples and government buildings stood around the Forum. After about 150 BC, gladiatorial games were held in the Forum and temporary wooden stands were erected in which spectators could sit.

233 One fight took place in a swivelling arena. In 53 BC, the politician Gaius Scribonius Curio put on a gladiator show and impressed the crowd by staging two plays in back-to-back theatres. The theatres swivelled around to form an arena for a small gladiator show. The crowd loved the new idea and Curio went on to win several elections.

234 The first purpose-built arena had the wrong name carved on it. In 29 BC an amphitheatre (an open-air building with rows of seats, one above the other) was built to the north of Rome by the politician Titus Statilius Taurus. The amphitheatre was built of stone and timber to replace temporary wooden stands in the Forum. Taurus wanted to impress Emperor Augustus so he carved the name 'Augustus' over the entrance.

▼ The name Augustus dominated the entrance to the arena built by Taurus.

AUGUSTUS

235 Every arena had the same layout. Arenas were oval with an entrance at each end. The gladiators came into the arena through one entrance, and the other was reserved for servants and for carrying out any dead gladiators. The editor sat in a special section of the seating called the tribunal editoris, which was on the north side in the shade.

TRUE OR FALSE?

1. The cattle market was the largest open space in Rome.
2. At first spectators watched from shops and temples.
3. Some arenas were round, some oval and some square.

Answers:
1. FALSE The Forum was the largest open space in Rome.
2. TRUE Early gladiatorial fights took place in the cattle market and spectators watched from nearby buildings. 3. FALSE All arenas were oval.

▼ All gladiatorial stadiums were oval in shape, with blocks of seating rising from the central arena.

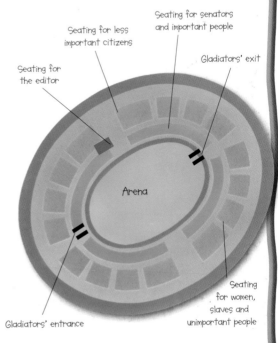

Seating for less important citizens

Seating for senators and important people

Gladiators' exit

Seating for the editor

Arena

Seating for women, slaves and unimportant people

Gladiators' entrance

The mighty Colosseum

236 **The Colosseum was named after a statue.** The official name of the Colosseum was the Flavian Amphitheatre, named after the Flavian dynasty of emperors who ordered it to be built. Most ordinary Romans called it the Colosseum because it was built next to the Colossus, a 30-metre-tall statue of Emperor Nero.

Wooden masts

Awning

▶ The Colosseum had complex underground passageways in which gladiators and wild animals were kept before they appeared in the games.

237 **The Colosseum was built on a marsh.** When Emperor Vespasian Flavian ordered building work to begin on the Colosseum in AD 72, there was only one piece of land large enough in Rome that had not already been built on. This was an area of marsh between the river Tiber and the emperor's palace. Before building work could begin the marsh had to be drained.

Stairs leading to seating areas

Underground entrance to arena

238 **The Colosseum could seat 50,000 spectators.** The huge seating area was divided into more than 80 sections. Each section had a separate door and flight of steps that led to the outside of the Colosseum. It is thought that the entire audience could have left in less than 15 minutes of the end of the show. The standing room at the top was reserved for slaves and may have held another 4000 people.

239 **The Colosseum was probably the largest building in the world.** It was finished in AD 80 and the outer walls stood over 46 metres tall and covered an area 194 metres long by 160 metres wide. The walls were covered in stone, but most of the structure was made of brick or concrete.

240 **The first games in the Colosseum lasted 100 days.** The Colosseum was finished during the reign of Emperor Titus. He wanted to show that he was the most generous man ever to live in Rome, so he organized gladiatorial games to last for 100 days. Thousands of gladiators and animals fought in these games, which some people thought were the finest ever staged in Rome.

Tiered seating

Trapdoors

Arena floor

Network of corridors and machinery beneath arena floor

109

Who were the gladiators?

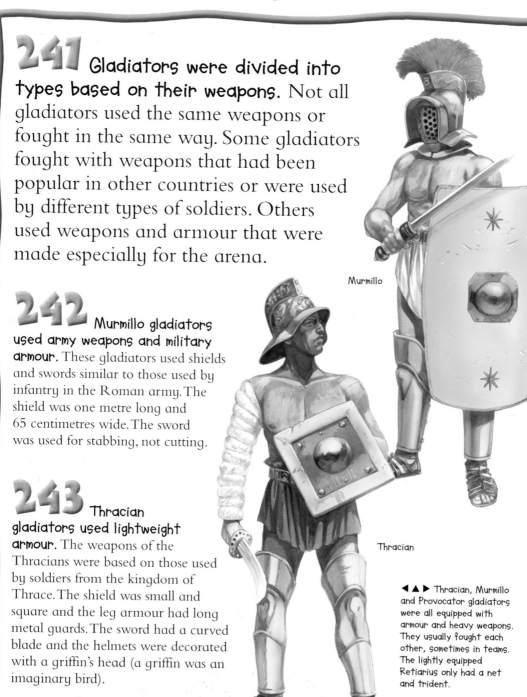

241 **Gladiators were divided into types based on their weapons.** Not all gladiators used the same weapons or fought in the same way. Some gladiators fought with weapons that had been popular in other countries or were used by different types of soldiers. Others used weapons and armour that were made especially for the arena.

Murmillo

242 **Murmillo gladiators used army weapons and military armour.** These gladiators used shields and swords similar to those used by infantry in the Roman army. The shield was one metre long and 65 centimetres wide. The sword was used for stabbing, not cutting.

243 **Thracian gladiators used lightweight armour.** The weapons of the Thracians were based on those used by soldiers from the kingdom of Thrace. The shield was small and square and the leg armour had long metal guards. The sword had a curved blade and the helmets were decorated with a griffin's head (a griffin was an imaginary bird).

Thracian

◄▲► Thracian, Murmillo and Provocator gladiators were all equipped with armour and heavy weapons. They usually fought each other, sometimes in teams. The lightly equipped Retiarius only had a net and trident.

244 Provocator gladiators wore the heaviest armour of all gladiators. They had a breastplate that protected the chest, a round helmet and leg armour that reached above the knees. The shield was about 80 centimetres long and 60 centimetres wide. They used a short, stabbing sword with a straight blade.

Retiarius

Provocator

MAKE A SHIELD

You will need:
cardboard scissors
string coloured paints

1. Take the sheet of cardboard and cut out a rectangular shape with rounded corners.
2. Ask an adult to make a pair of holes close to each long side and tie string through them to make handles.
3. Paint the front of the shield with a bright, colourful design like those in this book.

245 Retiarius gladiators had a fishing net and trident. These gladiators wore very little armour. They relied on speed and skill to escape attacks from heavily equipped gladiators, such as the provocator gladiators. The fishing net was used to try to trip or entangle an opponent. The trident, a spear with three points, was usually used by fishermen.

Special fighters

◀ The equite gladiators began their combat on horseback, but if one fell off his horse, the other had to fight on foot as well.

246 Equite gladiators were equipped in the same way as the cavalry in the Roman army. They used a small leather shield, a medium-length sword and a lance about 2.5 metres long. Only the helmet was different from that of the army. The army helmet had an open face and no brim. Whenever these gladiators appeared in a show they were the first to fight.

247 Female gladiators were rare. They first appeared around AD 55 in Rome as a novelty act. They fought only against other women or animals. Female gladiators were banned in AD 200.

▲ Female gladiators fought in the same style as the male gladiators.

248

The andabatae (an-dab-AH-tie) fought blindfolded. The Romans loved anything new or unusual. Andabatae gladiators wore helmets with no eye-holes. They listened carefully for sounds of their opponent, then attacked with two swords. Sometimes the andabatae fought on horseback.

249

British gladiators fought from chariots. Known as the essedarii (ess-e-DAH-ree-ee), meaning chariot-man, these gladiators first appeared after Julius Caesar invaded Britain in 55 BC. The first chariot gladiators were prisoners of war.

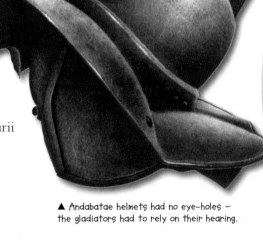

▲ Andabatae helmets had no eye-holes – the gladiators had to rely on their hearing.

ANDABATAE FIGHT

Recreate the combat of the andabatae with this game

You will need:
blindfold   four or more players

1. One player is the andabatae. Tie on the blindfold, making sure the player can see nothing.
2. Other players run around the andabatae calling out their name.
3. The andabatae tries to catch someone. When they catch a person, that person puts on the blindfold and becomes the andabatae. The game continues for as long as you like.

250

Special clowns who fought with wooden weapons were known as paegniarii (payeg-nee-AH-ree-ee). They appeared at shows during gaps between gladiator fights. They were skilled acrobats and would sometimes tell jokes or make fun of important people in the audience.

▶ The paegniarii used wooden weapons and put on comic displays to entertain the crowd between gladiator fights.

Recruiting gladiators

251 The first gladiators were household slaves. The will of the dead man who was being honoured by the games would name his slaves who were to fight. They were made to fight during the funeral. Those who were killed were then buried with their owner.

▲ Before a show, the names of the gladiators who were to fight were written on a scroll.

◀ When convicted, the name, crime and sentence of each criminal was inscribed on a tablet.

252 Criminals could be sent to the arena. The Romans did not have prisons so criminals were usually fined, flogged or executed. Men guilty of some crimes might be ordered to become gladiators for a set period of time – such as three years for robbery. These men would be given a tablet showing the details of their crime and sentence.

I DON'T BELIEVE IT!

When the lanista wanted to buy slaves to become gladiators, he would choose big, strong men. On average a gladiator was about 5 centimetres taller than an ordinary Roman.

253

Some gladiators were volunteers. These volunteers had often been former soldiers who wanted to earn money for their retirement. They signed up for a period of time or for a set number of fights and received a large payment of money if they survived.

255

Gladiators were recruited by the lanista. Every gladiator school was run by the lanista, the owner and chief trainer. The lanista decided who to recruit and how to train them. He would choose the strongest men to fight in heavy armour and the quickest men to fight as retiarius gladiators.

◀ Slaves for sale were paraded in front of potential buyers. They were sold to the highest bidder.

254

Strong slaves were sold to become gladiators. In ancient Rome, slaves were treated as the property of their owners and had no human rights at all. If a man wanted to raise money, he might sell a slave. The lanista would pay a high price for strong male slaves. Many young slaves were also sold to become gladiators.

▶ The price of slaves varied, but a slave might cost about the same as an average workman's wages for a year.

Learning to fight

256 **Gladiators lived in a special training school called a ludus.** Most early schools were located near Naples, but they later moved to Rome. Some schools specialized in a particular type of gladiator, but others trained all types. The school was run by the lanista, but some were owned by wealthy noblemen.

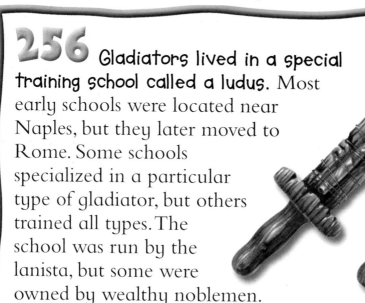

▲ Wooden training swords were the same size as real weapons.

257 **Gladiators trained with wooden weapons.** The weapons made sure that gladiators were not seriously injured during training. It also made it more difficult for gladiators to organize a rebellion, as Spartacus had done. Some wooden weapons were bound with heavy lead weights so that when gladiators fought with normal weapons they could fight for longer.

258 **A special oath was taken by trainee gladiators.** The sacred oath (promise) was taken in front of a shrine to the gods. The oath made the gladiator obey the lanista without question or endure branding, flogging, chains or death. Gladiators were allowed to keep any prize money they won.

▲ Most arenas and gladiator schools had a small shrine dedicated to the war god Mars.

259 New trainees fought against a wooden post called a palus. A trainer known as a doctor taught the recruits how to use their weapons and shields to strike at the 2-metre-high wooden post. Only when the basic tactics had been learned did the recruits practise against other gladiators.

▲ Gladiators trained for several hours every day, being instructed on fighting techniques by retired gladiators and more experienced men.

260 The buildings of a gladiator school were constructed around a square training ground. This was where the gladiators did most of their training, exercises and other activities. Around the training ground were rooms where the gladiators lived. Recruits slept in dormitories, but fully trained gladiators had their own rooms.

Armour, shields and helmets

261 **Gladiator helmets were decorated with colourful plumes and crests.** These were made from coloured feathers or dyed horsehair and made the gladiators look taller and bigger. Sometimes gladiators fought in teams and wore colours to show which team they belonged to.

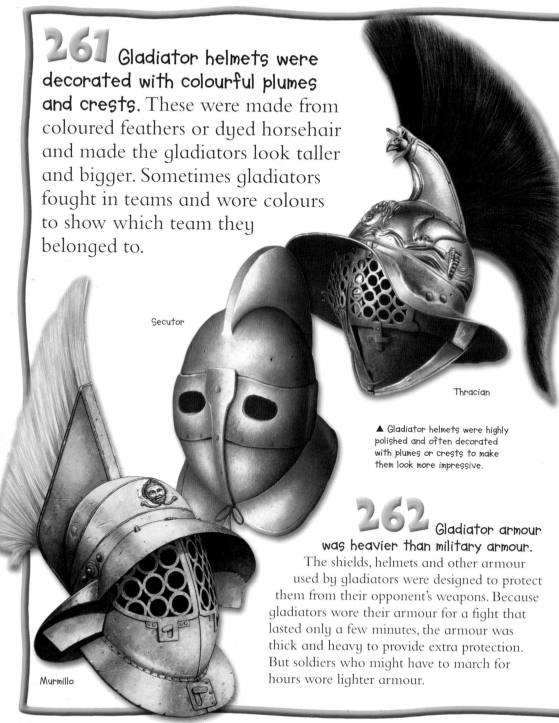

Secutor

Thracian

▲ Gladiator helmets were highly polished and often decorated with plumes or crests to make them look more impressive.

262 **Gladiator armour was heavier than military armour.** The shields, helmets and other armour used by gladiators were designed to protect them from their opponent's weapons. Because gladiators wore their armour for a fight that lasted only a few minutes, the armour was thick and heavy to provide extra protection. But soldiers who might have to march for hours wore lighter armour.

Murmillo

263 Some armour was covered with gold.

Most gladiator armour was decorated with carvings and reliefs of gods such as Mars, god of war, or Victory, goddess of success. These decorations were often coated with thin sheets of pure gold.

264 Padded armour was worn on the arms and legs.

Thick layers of cloth and padding gave protection from glancing blows from the weapons or from being hit by the shield of the opponent.

▲ Gladiator shields were painted and even decorated with gold to impress the audience.

Leather binding

Cloth padding

▲ Arms and legs were often covered with layers of woollen cloth tied on with leather bindings.

265 The body was usually left without any armour at all.

This meant that a single blow could kill them, or injure them so seriously that they had to ask for mercy. Gladiators needed to be skilful with both weapons and shields to survive.

I DON'T BELIEVE IT!

Gladiator helmets were very heavy — they weighed about 7 kilograms, twice as much as an army helmet!

A day in the life...

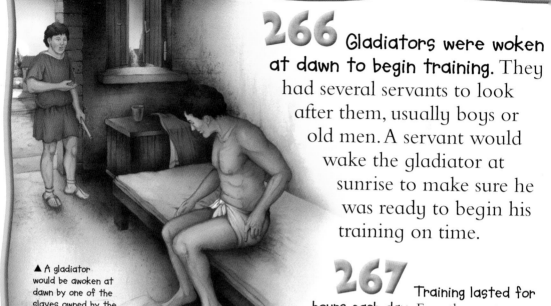

266 Gladiators were woken at dawn to begin training. They had several servants to look after them, usually boys or old men. A servant would wake the gladiator at sunrise to make sure he was ready to begin his training on time.

▲ A gladiator would be awoken at dawn by one of the slaves owned by the training school.

267 Training lasted for hours each day. Even the most experienced gladiator began his day practising weapon strokes at a wooden post. This allowed the fighter to warm up ready for the more serious training later in the day. Gladiators had special plain armour and blunt weapons to use when training.

GLADIATOR MEAL
Ask an adult to help you prepare this gladiator meal.
You will need:
60 g rolled porridge oats
400 ml water pinch of salt
50 g ham 5 dried figs
2 tbsp olive oil
1 tsp dried rosemary.
1. Chop the ham and figs. Fry in the olive oil and rosemary.
2. Place the oats, water and salt in a saucepan. Bring to the boil, then simmer for 5 minutes.
3. When the oats have thickened, scatter over the ham and figs.

◀ A stout wooden post about 2 metres tall was used for the more basic training exercises.

◀ Gladiators were given simple, but nutritious food such as porridge, carrots and sausages to keep them fit and healthy.

270 Barley porridge was the usual food of gladiators, but they also ate meats, fruits and vegetables. The Romans believed that barley was a highly nutritious food that helped to build up muscles. The owner of the gladiator school did not waste money on fancy foods, but provided plain and healthy meals.

268 Gladiators received regular massages. Romans knew that massages would help to ease stiff joints or relax muscles. Massages could be very helpful to old injuries. The gladiator school would employ at least one man who was an expert masseur to keep the gladiators in top condition.

▼ Gladiators were sometimes given treatment by masseurs, doctors and other specialists who looked after their health.

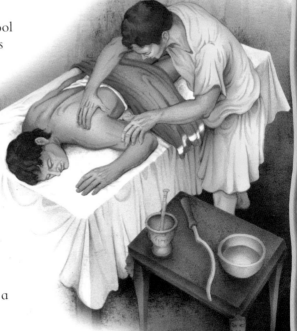

269 Older, retired gladiators trained the new recruits. Gladiators who survived long enough to win their freedom often found jobs at gladiator schools. They were expert fighters and knew many tricks and special moves. They trained the new recruits to be expert fighters. This would please the crowd, and give the gladiator a better chance of surviving.

Get ready for the games

271 **The first decision was how much money to spend.** The man who staged a munus, or gladiatorial games, was known as the editor. A munus was an expensive event but most editors wanted to put on the most impressive show possible. They would spend as much money as they could spare.

272 **The editor would choose different features for his show.** A lanista would be hired to organize the show. Together, they would decide how many gladiators would fight and how many musicians and other performers were needed. The lanista would make sure the event was a success.

▲ Musicians and dancers were popular at gladiator shows. Shows often included a parade of entertainers before the gladiators.

273 **A dead gladiator cost more than a wounded one.** The editor would sign a contract with the lanista. This set down everything that would appear at the munus and the cost. If a gladiator was killed, a special payment was made so that the lanista could buy and train a replacement. Many editors granted mercy to a wounded man to avoid paying extra.

QUIZ

1. Who decided on the features for a gladiatorial show?
2. Did the editor of the games wear his everyday toga or expensive clothing?
3. Was a toga with purple edges worn by noblemen or ordinary citizens?

Answers:
1. The editor and lanista.
2. He hired special clothing to wear.
3. Noblemen.

274
Everything was hired — even the clothes worn by the organizer. The editor would hire expensive clothes and jewellery for himself and his family. He wanted to make sure that they looked their best when they appeared at the games. The editor wanted to impress his fellow citizens and make sure they would vote for him.

275
The star of the show was the editor. Everything was arranged so that the editor of the games looked as important as possible. As well as wearing special clothes, he was given the most prominent seat in the amphitheatre and all the gladiators and other performers bowed to him. He was paying for the show and wanted to make sure he got all the credit.

▼ Smart clothes were hired for the editor and all his family so that they could show off to the audience.

A laurel wreath signified an honour granted by the Roman government

Gold jewellery indicated a family's wealth

Brightly coloured silk from China showed wealth and sophistication

A toga was a special item of clothing that indicated the rank within society of the man wearing it

Purple was the most expensive dye in ancient Rome

Showtime!

276 **Advertising for the show began days beforehand.** The lanista sent out slaves to paint signs on walls, while others shouted announcements on the street. The slaves told people when and where the show was and what it included. They also told them the name of the editor of the show.

277 **The show began with a parade, which was led into the arena by the editor.** He was dressed in beautiful clothes and often rode in a chariot. Behind him came the musicians playing lively tunes. Then came the gladiators, each followed by a slave who carried the gladiator's weapons and armour. Then came statues of the war god Mars and other gods. Finally the servants, referees and other officials entered the arena.

278 **Gladiators were carefully paired against each other.** Before the show began, the editor and lanista would decide which gladiators would fight each other. The show would start with beginners fighting each other, with the expert veterans appearing towards the end of the show. The results would be shouted out by a herald and written on a sign, or tabella, at one end of the arena.

280
The probatio was a crucial ceremony. Before the first fight of the show, the editor and lanista would enter the arena for the probatio. This ceremony involved the men testing the weapons and armour to be used in the show. Swords were tested by slicing up vegetables, and armour by being hit with clubs.

◀ Each gladiator show began with a grand parade of everyone involved in the show, led by the editor in a chariot.

279
Musicians performed first. The band included trumpets, curved horns and the hydraulis. This was a loud instrument like a modern church organ. The musicians entertained the crowd between fights and played music during the show ceremonies.

TRUE OR FALSE?

1. The hydraulis was an instrument like a modern trumpet.
2. Weapons were tested before the show to make sure they were sharp.
3. Gladiators wore their armour during the opening parade.

Answers:
1. FALSE The hydraulis was an instrument like a modern organ. 2. TRUE Weapons were tested during the probatio ceremony. 3. FALSE Slaves carried the armour behind the gladiators.

Water fights

281 **Some gladiatorial shows took place on water.** The most impressive of all were the naumachiae, or sea fights. For these shows, an artificial lake 557 metres long by 536 metres wide was dug beside the river Tiber. Small warships were brought up the river and launched on the lake when a sea fight was due to take place.

282 **Naval fights were recreations of real battles.** In 2 BC, Emperor Augustus staged a naumachia that recreated a battle fought 400 years earlier between the Greeks and the Persians. Emperor Titus staged a battle that originally started between the Greeks and Egyptians. These battles did not always end with the same winner as the real battle.

▼ Recreated naval battles were extremely expensive to stage, so didn't take place very often.

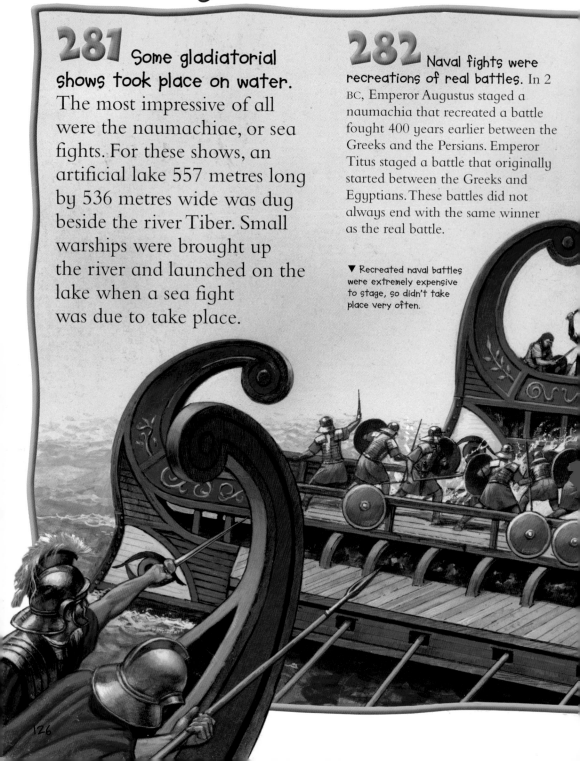

283 The first naval gladiators did not try to kill each other.
The first of the sea battles were staged by Julius Caesar to celebrate a naval victory. The show was designed to impress the audience with the skills of the sailors and the way Caesar had won his victory.

284 One naval show involved 19,000 men.
Emperor Claudius staged a sea battle on Lake Fucino. The men fighting were not sailors or gladiators but criminals condemned to death. Most of the men died and any survivors were sent to work as slaves.

285 The Colosseum in Rome could be flooded for naval fights.
When the Colosseum was first built it had special pipes that could fill the arena with water and then drain it away again. The flooded arena was used for fights between special miniature warships crewed by gladiators. Later, the pipes were replaced by trapdoors and stage scenery.

I DON'T BELIEVE IT!
On one occasion, gladiators took one look at the poor condition of the warships and refused to board them.

Wild animal hunts

286 The first wild animal show was to celebrate a military victory. In 164 BC Rome defeated the powerful North African city of Carthage. The victorious general, Publius Cornelius Scipio, was given the nickname Africanus. He brought back to Rome hundreds of African wild animals, such as elephants, crocodiles and lions. After parading the animals through the streets, he included them in his gladiatorial games.

▲ This ancient mosaic shows the capture of wild animals, such as lions and gazelles. They were then shipped to Rome to fight in the arenas.

287 One elephant hunt went badly wrong. In 79 BC General Gnaeus Pompey staged a wild elephant hunt with 20 elephants in a temporary arena in Rome. The crowd was protected by a tall iron fence, but two of the elephants charged at the fence, smashing it down. The elephants were quickly killed by hunters, but several people were injured.

288 The design of the arena changed to make it safer for the crowds. As the wild animal shows became more popular the need to keep the watching crowd safe meant changes to the arena had to be made. The arena was sunk about 3 metres into the ground and surrounded by a vertical wall of smooth stone. No animal could leap up the wall or break it down, so the spectators were safe from attack.

289

Some animal shows were fantastic and strange. The Romans loved to see animals fighting each other. Sometimes a group of lions or wolves would be set to attack zebras or deer. At other times two hunting animals would be made to fight each other. They were often chained together to encourage them to fight. Some pairings were very odd. A snake was set against a lion, a seal set to fight a wolf or a bull against a bear.

290

Lions were set to fight tigers. One of the most popular animal fights was when a lion was set against a tiger. So many lions and tigers were sent to Rome to die in the fights that they became extinct in some areas of North Africa and the Middle East.

I DON'T BELIEVE IT!

The Romans loved watching animals that had been trained to perform tricks. One animal trainer put on shows in which an ape drove a chariot pulled by camels.

▼ A wild tiger attacks a gladiator, as seen in the 2000 movie *Gladiator*. Wild animals were part of most arena shows.

Outside Rome

291 More gladiators fought in southern Italy than in Rome. The idea of gladiatorial fights came from Campania, the area of Italy around Naples. For hundreds of years, the gladiator schools in Campania produced the best-trained gladiators and had more than anywhere else. One school had over 5000 gladiators training at one time.

292 The city of London had a small arena for gladiatorial games and other events. It stood inside the city walls beside the army fortress, near what is now St Paul's Cathedral. The 30-metre-long amphitheatre was built of stone and timber and could seat around 4000 spectators. St Albans, Chester and Caerleon also had amphitheatres.

▼ The arena at Pompeii. The oval shape, banked seating and two exits were the common design for all arenas.

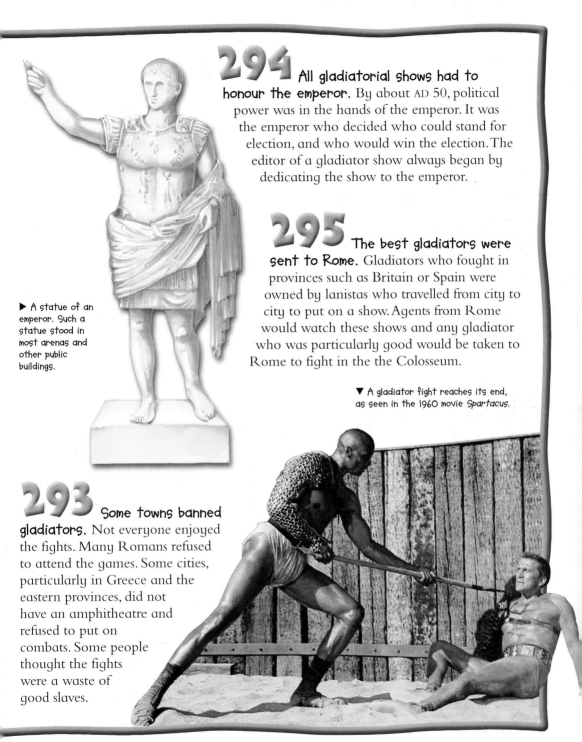

294 All gladiatorial shows had to honour the emperor. By about AD 50, political power was in the hands of the emperor. It was the emperor who decided who could stand for election, and who would win the election. The editor of a gladiator show always began by dedicating the show to the emperor.

▶ A statue of an emperor. Such a statue stood in most arenas and other public buildings.

295 The best gladiators were sent to Rome. Gladiators who fought in provinces such as Britain or Spain were owned by lanistas who travelled from city to city to put on a show. Agents from Rome would watch these shows and any gladiator who was particularly good would be taken to Rome to fight in the the Colosseum.

▼ A gladiator fight reaches its end, as seen in the 1960 movie *Spartacus*.

293 Some towns banned gladiators. Not everyone enjoyed the fights. Many Romans refused to attend the games. Some cities, particularly in Greece and the eastern provinces, did not have an amphitheatre and refused to put on combats. Some people thought the fights were a waste of good slaves.

The last gladiators

▲ A scene from the 2000 movie *Gladiator*. The bloodshed in gladiator fights appalled some Romans.

296 **Gladiatorial games became less and less popular.** Seneca, a wise man and a great thinker, wrote that attending the games made Romans more cruel and inhuman than they had been before. The writer Artemidorus of Daldis said that the games were dishonourable, cruel and wicked. However most Romans approved of the games and enjoyed watching them.

297 **In AD 324, Christian bishops tried to ban gladiatorial fights.** After AD 250, Christianity became popular in the Roman Empire. Christians believed that the fights were sinful and they asked Emperor Constantine I to ban the fights. He banned private games, but allowed state games to continue.

QUIZ

1. Which philosopher thought watching gladiator fights made people cruel?
2. Which emperor closed down the gladiator schools in Rome?
3. Which emperor banned private gladiatorial games?

Answers:
1. Seneca. 2. Emperor Honorius. 3. Emperor Constantine I.

298
In AD 366 Pope Damasus used gladiators to murder rival churchmen. When Pope Liberius died the cardinals of Rome could not agree on a successor. Followers who wanted Ursinus to be the next pope were meeting in the church of St Maria Trastevere when Damasus hired a gang of gladiators to attack them. The gladiators broke into the church and killed 137 people. Damasus then became pope.

299
The Christian monk Telemachus was the first to stop a gladiator fight. During a show in the Colosseum in AD 404, Telemachus forced apart two fighting gladiators. He made a speech asking for the shows to stop, but angry spectators killed him. Emperor Honorius then closed down all the gladiator schools in Rome.

▲ Heavily armed gladiators were sometimes hired by ambitious politicians and churchmen to murder their rivals.

300
The last gladiators fought in around AD 445. In AD 410, the city of Rome was captured by a tribe of barbarians. The Roman Empire was falling to pieces. People were too busy trying to escape invasions or to earn a living to organize gladiatorial fights.

◀ The monk Telemachus managed to stop a gladiator fight, but paid for his actions with his life.

133

What is a mummy?

301 A mummy is a dead body that has not rotted away. Natural mummies are accidents of nature, made by freezing, drying or waterlogging. Artificial mummies are made on purpose, by people who have used different ways to preserve bodies. The best known artificial mummies were made in ancient Egypt. Long ago, travellers from Persia (modern-day Iran) thought that a sticky black substance, called bitumen, was used to make Egyptian mummies. The Persian word for bitumen was *mummia*, and from this comes the English word 'mummy'.

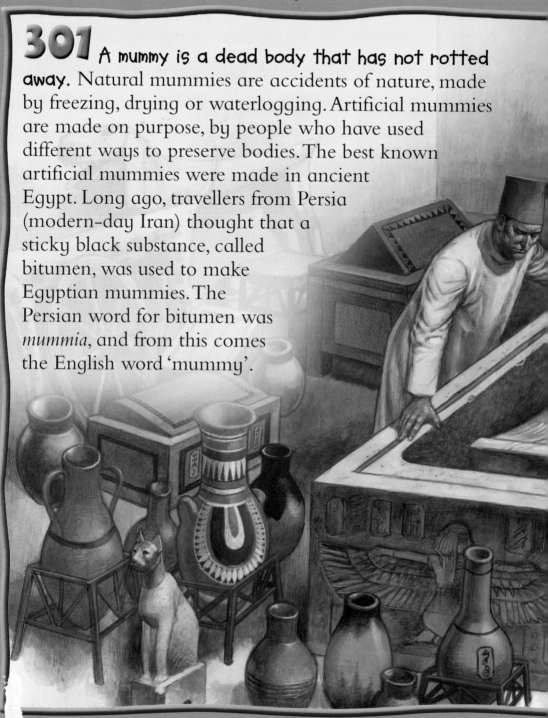

▲ The 3300-year-old mummy of Egyptian pharaoh Tutankhamun was discovered in 1922 by Howard Carter. This is a good example of an artificial mummy.

The first mummies

302 The first artificial mummies were made 7000 years ago by the Chinchorro people of South America. These people are named after a place in Chile. Here, scientists discovered traces of the way the Chinchorro lived. They were a fishing people who lived in small groups along the coast of the Pacific Ocean.

▼ A clay mask was sometimes placed over the face of a Chinchorro mummy.

303 It is thought that the Chinchorro made mummies because they believed in life after death. They tried to make a mummy look as lifelike as possible, which shows they did not want the person's body to rot away. Perhaps they thought the dead could live again if their bodies were preserved.

304 To make a mummy, the Chinchorro first removed all of a dead person's insides. The skin and flesh were then taken off the bones, which were left to dry. Then sticks were tied to the arm, leg and spine bones to hold them together. White mud was spread over the skeleton to build a body shape. The face skin was put back in place, and patches of skin were added to the body. When the mud was dry, it was painted black or red.

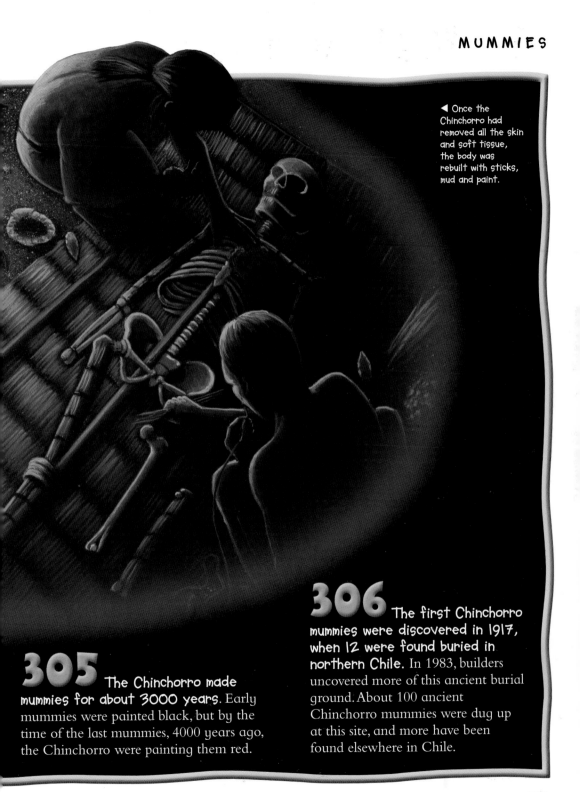

◄ Once the Chinchorro had removed all the skin and soft tissue, the body was rebuilt with sticks, mud and paint.

306 The first Chinchorro mummies were discovered in 1917, when 12 were found buried in northern Chile. In 1983, builders uncovered more of this ancient burial ground. About 100 ancient Chinchorro mummies were dug up at this site, and more have been found elsewhere in Chile.

305 The Chinchorro made mummies for about 3000 years. Early mummies were painted black, but by the time of the last mummies, 4000 years ago, the Chinchorro were painting them red.

Iceman of Europe

307 Europe's oldest human mummy is known as the Iceman. He died about 5300 years ago, at the end of the Stone Age. His mummy was discovered by hikers in northern Italy in 1991. They found it lying face down in an icy glacier.

309 When the Iceman was alive, arrows had sharp points made from flint (a type of stone). It was a flint arrowhead that injured the Iceman, piercing his clothes and entering his left shoulder. This arrow caused a deep wound. The Iceman pulled the long arrow shaft out, but the arrowhead remained inside his body. This injury would have made the Iceman weak, eventually causing him to die.

◄ The Iceman is the oldest complete human mummy ever to be found. He is so well preserved, even his eyes are still visible.

308 The Iceman mummy was found high up in the mountains, where it is very cold. At first, people thought that he was a shepherd, or a hunter on the search for food – or even a traveller on a journey. Then in 2001, an arrowhead was found in the Iceman's left shoulder. He might have fled into the mountains to escape danger.

310 The mummy's clothes were also preserved by the ice. For the first time, scientists saw how a Stone Age person actually dressed. The Iceman wore leggings and shoes made from leather, a goatskin coat, a bearskin hat and a cape made from woven grass. These would have kept the Iceman warm in the cold climate.

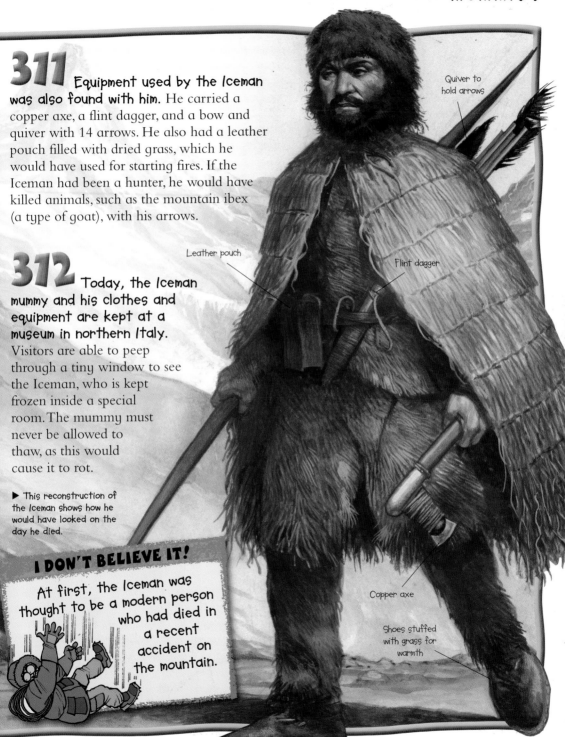

311
Equipment used by the Iceman was also found with him. He carried a copper axe, a flint dagger, and a bow and quiver with 14 arrows. He also had a leather pouch filled with dried grass, which he would have used for starting fires. If the Iceman had been a hunter, he would have killed animals, such as the mountain ibex (a type of goat), with his arrows.

312
Today, the Iceman mummy and his clothes and equipment are kept at a museum in northern Italy. Visitors are able to peep through a tiny window to see the Iceman, who is kept frozen inside a special room. The mummy must never be allowed to thaw, as this would cause it to rot.

▶ This reconstruction of the Iceman shows how he would have looked on the day he died.

Quiver to hold arrows

Leather pouch

Flint dagger

Copper axe

Shoes stuffed with grass for warmth

I DON'T BELIEVE IT!
At first, the Iceman was thought to be a modern person who had died in a recent accident on the mountain.

139

Bog bodies

313 Lots of mummies have been found in the peat bogs of northern Europe. Peat is a soily substance that is formed from plants that have fallen into pools of water. The plants sink to the bottom and are slowly turned into peat. If a dead body is placed in a bog, it may be preserved as a mummy. This is because there is little oxygen or bacteria to rot the body.

I DON'T BELIEVE IT!

When Tollund Man was found, scientists could only save his head. His body was left to dry until only the bones were left.

314 Bog bodies, or mummies, are usually found when peat is dug up. One of the best known bodies was dug up at Tollund, Denmark, in 1950. Tollund Man, as he is known, died 2300 years ago. Around his neck was a leather noose. He was hanged, perhaps as a sacrifice to his gods, and then thrown in the bog. Over the years his face was perfectly preserved, right down to the whiskers on his chin!

▶ The face of Tollund Man is so well preserved, he looks as if he is sleeping.

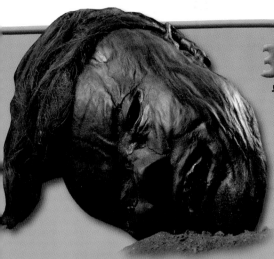

316 Grauballe Man was also found in a peat bog in Denmark. He was discovered by peat workers near the village of Grauballe in 1852. About 2300 years ago, the man's throat was cut and he bled to death. His body was thrown into a bog, where it was preserved until its discovery.

▲ The head of Grauballe Man. Like all bog bodies, his skin has turned brown due to the acids in the bog.

315 Bog bodies have also been discovered in Germany. At Windeby, the body of a teenage girl was found. The girl, who died 1900 years ago, was wearing a blindfold. It seems she was taken to the bog, her eyes were covered, and then she was drowned. A heavy rock and branches were put on top of her body, so it sank to the bottom of the bog.

▶ The mummy of Windeby Girl revealed that some of her hair had been cut off, or shaved, at the time of her death.

317 From the Netherlands comes the bog body of another teenage girl. Known as Yde (*ay-de*) Girl, she was stabbed, strangled and then dumped in a bog around 1900 years ago. A medical artist made a copy of her skull, then covered it with wax to rebuild her face. The model shows scientists how Yde Girl may have looked when she was alive.

Lindow Man

318 A bog body of a man was found in north-west England in 1984. It was discovered by peat cutters at Lindow Moss, Cheshire. The mummy was named 'Lindow Man', but a local newspaper nicknamed it 'Pete Marsh' because a peat bog is a wet, marshy place! Lindow Man is now on display at the British Museum, London.

319 Lindow Man was about 20 years old when he died. His short life came to an end around 1900 years ago. After his death, his body was put in a bog, where it sank without trace until its discovery by the peat cutters.

▼ The body of Lindow Man was squashed flat by the weight of the peat on top of it.

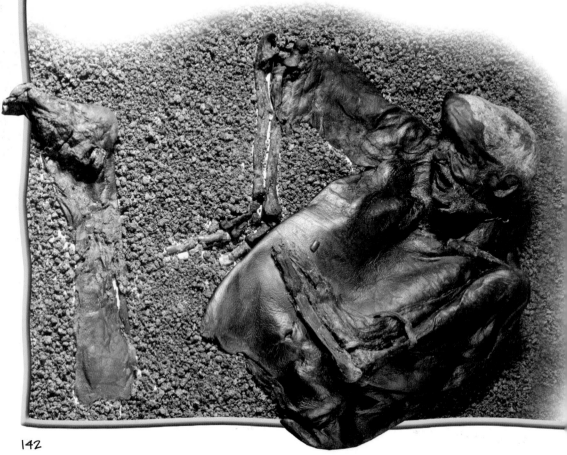

320 Lindow Man did not die peacefully. Before he died, he ate food with poisonous mistletoe in it. It's impossible to say if the poison was put there on purpose, or by accident. The marks on his body tell the story of his last moments alive. Someone hit him hard on the head, a cord was tightened around his neck and he was strangled. Then, to make sure he was dead, his throat was cut.

321 It took four years to find most of Lindow Man's body. The machine used to cut the peat had sliced it into pieces, which were found at different times. His top half, from the waist up, was found in 1984, and four years later his left leg turned up. His right leg is missing, possibly still buried in the peat bog.

▲ In this reconstruction, Lindow Man eats a meal containing burnt bread. This may have been part of a ceremony in which he was sacrificed to the gods.

I DON'T BELIEVE IT!

Visitors to the British Museum have come up with names for Lindow Man, including Sludge Man and Man in the Toilet!

322 In Lindow Man's time, gifts were given to the gods. The greatest gift was a human sacrifice, which is what may have happened to Lindow Man. After eating a meal mixed with mistletoe, he was killed and put in a bog. People thought he was leaving this world and entering the world of the gods.

Mummies of ancient Egypt

▲ Even pet dogs were mummified in ancient Egypt.

323 **The most famous mummies were made in ancient Egypt.** The Egyptians were skilled embalmers (mummy-makers). Pharaohs (rulers of Egypt) and ordinary people were made into mummies, along with many kinds of animal.

▲ Two people walk through the Field of Reeds, which was the ancient Egyptian name for paradise.

324 **Mummies were made because the Egyptians thought that the dead needed their bodies in a new life after death.** They believed a person would live forever in paradise, but only if their body was saved. Every Egyptian wanted to travel to paradise after death. This is why they went to such trouble to preserve the bodies of the dead.

325 **Ancient Egypt's first mummies were made by nature.** When a person died, their body was buried in a pit in the desert sand. The person was buried with objects to use in the next life. Because the sand was hot and dry, the flesh did not rot. Instead, the flesh and skin dried and shrivelled until they were stretched over the bones. The body had been mummified. Egypt's natural mummies date from around 3500 BC.

327 The ancient Egyptians made their first artificial mummies around 3400 BC. The last mummies were made around AD 400. This means the Egyptians were making mummies for 4000 years! They stopped making them because as the Christian religion spread to Egypt, mummy-making came to be seen as a pagan (non-Christian) practice.

◀ This man died 5200 years ago in Egypt. His body slowly dried out in the hot, desert conditions, and became a natural mummy.

326 When an old grave was found, perhaps by robbers who wanted to steal the grave goods, they got a surprise. Instead of digging up a skeleton, they uncovered a dried-up body that still looked like a person! This might have started the ancient Egyptians thinking – could they find a way to preserve bodies themselves?

▶ Many Egyptian coffins were shaped like a person and beautifully painted and decorated.

Egypt's first mummy

328 The ancient Egyptians told a myth about how the very first mummy was made. The story was about Osiris, who was ruler of Egypt. It explained how Osiris became the first mummy, and because it had happened to him, people wanted to follow his example and be mummified when they died.

329 The story begins with the murder of Osiris. He had a wicked brother called Seth, and one day Seth tricked Osiris into lying inside a box. The box was really a coffin. Seth shut the lid and threw the coffin into the river Nile, and Osiris drowned. Seth killed his brother because he was jealous of him – he felt the people of Egypt did not love him as much as they loved Osiris.

330 Isis was married to Osiris, and she could not bear to be parted from him. She searched throughout Egypt for his body, and when she found it, she brought it home. Isis knew that Seth would be angry if he found out what she had done, and so she hid the dead body of Osiris.

QUIZ

1. Who killed Osiris?
2. Who was the wife of Osiris?
3. How many pieces did Seth cut Osiris into?
4. Which three gods helped Isis?
5. What did Osiris become in the afterlife?

Answers:
1. Seth 2. Isis 3. 14
4. Ra, Anubis, Thoth
5. King of the dead

▶ Isis, Anubis and Thoth rebuild the body of Osiris to make the first mummy.

331
However Seth found out, and he took the body of Osiris from its hiding place. Seth cut Osiris into 14 pieces, which he scattered far and wide across Egypt. At last, he thought, he had finally got rid of Osiris.

332
Seth might have destroyed Osiris, but he could not destroy the love that Isis had for him. Once again, Isis searched for Osiris. She turned herself into a kite (a bird of prey), and flew high above Egypt so she could look down upon the land to see where Seth had hidden the body parts of Osiris. One by one, Isis found the pieces of her husband's body, except for one, which was eaten by a fish.

333
Isis brought the pieces together. She wept at the sight of her husband's body. When Ra, the sun god, saw her tears, he sent the gods Anubis and Thoth to help her. Anubis wrapped the pieces of Osiris' body in cloth. Then Isis, Anubis and Thoth laid them out in the shape of Osiris and wrapped the whole body. The first mummy had been made. Isis kissed the mummy and Osiris was reborn, not to live in this world, but to live forever in the afterlife as king of the dead.

A very messy job

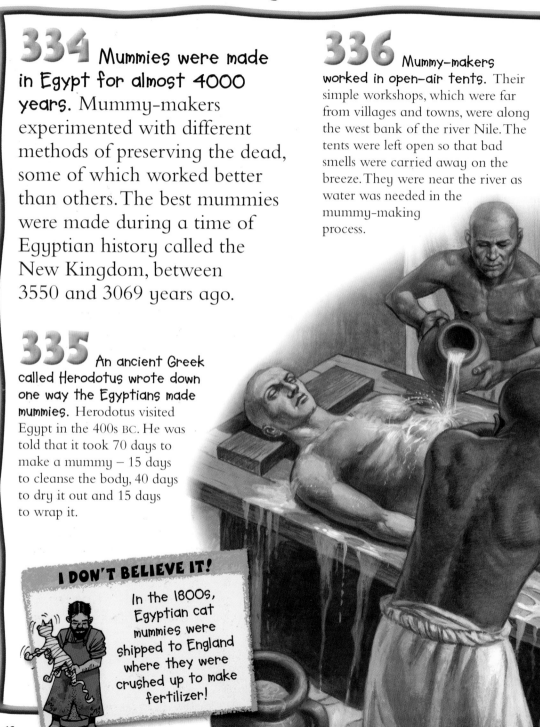

334 Mummies were made in Egypt for almost 4000 years. Mummy-makers experimented with different methods of preserving the dead, some of which worked better than others. The best mummies were made during a time of Egyptian history called the New Kingdom, between 3550 and 3069 years ago.

335 An ancient Greek called Herodotus wrote down one way the Egyptians made mummies. Herodotus visited Egypt in the 400s BC. He was told that it took 70 days to make a mummy – 15 days to cleanse the body, 40 days to dry it out and 15 days to wrap it.

336 Mummy-makers worked in open-air tents. Their simple workshops, which were far from villages and towns, were along the west bank of the river Nile. The tents were left open so that bad smells were carried away on the breeze. They were near the river as water was needed in the mummy-making process.

I DON'T BELIEVE IT!

In the 1800s, Egyptian cat mummies were shipped to England where they were crushed up to make fertilizer!

▶ To remove the brain, a metal hook was pushed up through the left nostril. It was then used to pull the brain out through the nose.

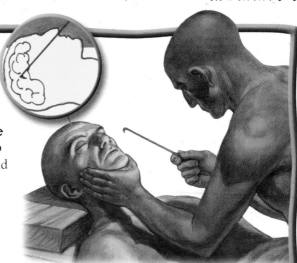

337
Mummy-making skills were handed down from one generation to the next. It was a job for men only, and it was a father's duty to train his son. A boy learned by watching his father at work. If his father worked as a slitter – the man who made the first cut in the body – his son also became a slitter.

338
The first 15 days of making a mummy involved cleaning the body. In the Place of Purification tent, the body was washed with salty water. It was then taken to the House of Beauty tent. Here, the brain was removed and thrown away. Then a slit was made in the left side of the body and the liver, lungs, intestines and stomach were taken out and kept.

339
The heart was left inside the body. The Egyptians thought the heart was the centre of intelligence. They believed it was needed to guide the person in the next life. If the heart was removed by mistake, it was put back inside. The kidneys were also left inside the body.

◀ A dead body was carefully washed with salty water before its organs were removed.

Drying the body

340 **After the insides had been taken out, the body was dried.** Mummy-makers used a special salt called natron to do the drying. The salt was a powdery-white mixture and was found along the edges of lakes in the north of Egypt. The natron was put into baskets, then taken to the mummy-makers.

343 **The liver, lungs, intestines and stomach were also dried.** Each of these organs was placed in a separate pottery bowl, and natron was piled on top. Just like the body, these organs were also left for 40 days, during which time the natron dried them out.

Bags of natron

341 **At the workshop, small linen bags were filled with natron.** The bags were packed into the empty body through the slit where the insides had been taken out. As well as the natron, rags, straw, dried grass and sawdust were also stuffed into the body. They helped to give the body its human shape.

Sawdust

Dried grass

▲ Some of the materials used by mummy-makers to stuff the bodies of mummies.

342 **Next, the body was placed on its back on a table and covered in a thick layer of natron.** No flesh was left exposed. The body was left to dry out under the natron for 40 days.

344 **Fisherman first used natron to dry the fish they caught.** They realized that natron's salty crystals sucked juices out of dead flesh, leaving it dry. Dried, or salted, fish did not rot. This was why the mummy-makers began to use natron to preserve the dead.

345 **During the 40 days of drying, the natron absorbed the body's juices.** At the end of this time, the mummy-makers scraped away the natron and removed the materials used to stuff the body. The dried body had lost about three-quarters of its original weight and was shrivelled, hard and blue-black in colour. It hardly looked like a body at all.

▲ The body was covered in natron, a kind of salt, to dry it out. Up to 225 kilograms were needed.

Wrapped from head to toe

346 The next job was to make the body appear lifelike. The body cavity was filled and the skin was rubbed with oil and spices to make it soft and sweet-smelling. Then it was given false eyes and a wig, and make-up was applied. Lastly, tree resin was poured over it. This set into a hard layer to stop mould growing.

347 The dried-out organs were wrapped in linen, then put into containers called canopic jars. The container with the baboon head (the god Hapi) held the lungs, and the stomach was put into the jackal-headed jar (the god Duamutef). The human-headed jar (the god Imseti) protected the liver, and the intestines were placed in the falcon-headed jar (the god Qebehsenuef).

Hapi

Imseti

◄ The four canopic jars represented the sons of the god Horus.

Duamutef

Qebehsenuef

348 The cut on the left side of the body was rarely stitched up. Instead, it was covered with a wax plaque. On the plaque was a design known as the Eye of Horus. The Egyptians believed it had the power to see evil and stop it from entering the body through the cut.

1. Head wrapped

Eye of Horus

349

In the final part of the process, the body was wrapped. It took 11 days to do this. The body was wrapped in strips of linen, 6 to 20 centimetres wide. There was a set way of wrapping the body, which always started with the head. Lastly, the body was covered with a sheet of linen, tied with linen bands.

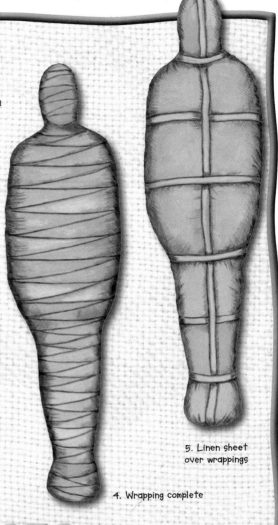

5. Linen sheet over wrappings

4. Wrapping complete

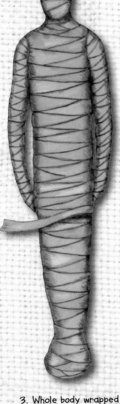

3. Whole body wrapped

▲ There was a five-stage sequence for wrapping the body, which always started with the head.

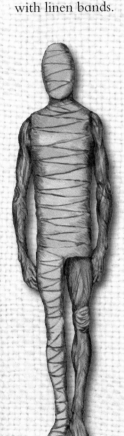

2. Limbs and torso wrapped

350

During the wrapping, amulets (lucky charms) were placed between the layers of linen. These protected the person from harm on their journey to the afterlife. Magic spells written on the wrappings were another form of protection. After it was wrapped, resin was poured over the mummy to make it waterproof. Last of all, it was given a face mask.

Tombs and tomb robbers

351 **The body was placed in a wooden coffin.** Simple coffins were made from planks of wood, and expensive ones were shaped like a person. They were decorated with spells. A picture on the inside of the coffin showed the route to the afterlife.

352 **The earliest pharaohs (kings) were buried in pyramid tombs.** The first pyramid was built about 2650 BC, for Pharaoh Djoser. For the next 800 years, all pharaohs were buried in pyramids. However robbers found their way into all of them. Later pharaohs were buried in tombs cut into a rocky valley, known as the Valley of the Kings. Robbers found many of these tombs too, but not all.

353

On the day of burial, the mummy was lifted out of its coffin and stood upright. A priest used a Y-shaped stone tool to touch the mummy's mouth, eyes, nose and ears. This was the Opening of the Mouth ceremony. It was done so that the person's speech, sight, hearing and smell came back to them for use in the next life.

▲ A priest (right) about to touch a mummy (left) in the Opening of the Mouth ceremony.

354

Mummies were buried with grave goods. These were items for the person to use in the next life. Ordinary people were buried with basic items, such as food and drink. Pharaohs and wealthy people were buried with everything they would need in their next life, such as furniture, clothes, weapons, jewellery and musical instruments.

355

Tombs were tempting places to robbers. They knew what was inside them, and took great risks to break in and steal the goods. Not even a mummy was safe – the tomb robbers smashed coffins open, and cut their way through the layers of linen wrappings to get at the masks, amulets and jewellery. Tomb robbery was a major crime, and if a robber was caught he was put to death.

◀ A funeral procession on its way to the Valley of the Kings. Oxen pulled the coffin on a wooden sledge shaped like a boat. This represented the deceased's journey to the next life.

Tutankhamun, the boy-king

▲ This model of Tutankhamun was buried with him in his tomb.

356 Tutankhamun is one of Egypt's most famous pharaohs. He became king in 1334 BC when he was eight years old. Because he was too young to carry out the important work of ruling Egypt, two of his ministers took charge. They were Ay, chief minister, and Horemheb, head of the army. They made decisions on Tutankhamun's behalf.

357 Tutankhamun was pharaoh for about nine years. He died when he was 17 years old. His body was mummified and buried in a tomb cut into the side of a valley. Many pharaohs were laid to rest in this valley, known as the Valley of the Kings. Tutankhamun was buried with valuables for use in the next life.

358 The tombs in the Valley of the Kings were meant to be secret. However robbers found them, and stole the precious items buried there. They found Tutankhamun's tomb, but were caught before they could do much damage. Years later, when the tomb of Rameses VI was being dug, rubble rolled down the valley and blocked the entrance to Tutankhamun's tomb. After that, it was forgotten about.

359

In 1922, British archaeologist Howard Carter discovered the tomb of Tutankhamun. He had spent years searching for it. Other archaeologists thought he was wasting his time. They said all the tombs in the valley had already been found. Carter refused to give up, and in November 1922 he found a stairway that led to the door of a tomb.

◀ Found covering the head and shoulders of Tutankhamun's mummy, this beautiful mask features a royal cobra and a vulture's head, representing the unification of Upper and Lower Egypt.

▲ Tutankhamun's throne. The back is decorated with a picture of the pharaoh, who is seated, and a princess.

360

Behind the door was a corridor. At the end of it was a second door, which Carter made a hole in. He peered through the hole, and said he could see 'wonderful things'. It took ten years to remove all the objects from the tomb — jewellery and a gold throne were among the treasures. A gold mask covered the king's head and shoulders. It was made of 10 kilograms of pure gold.

Magnificent mummies!

361 The mummy of pharaoh Rameses II was found in 1871. It had been buried in a tomb, but had been moved to prevent robbers finding it. Rameses II had bad teeth, probably caused by eating gritty bread. He was in his eighties when he died and had arthritis, which would have given him painful joints. In 1976 his mummy was sent to France for treatment to stop mould from damaging it.

362 Mummy 1770 is in the Manchester Museum, in the UK. This is a mummy of a teenage girl, whose real name is not known. Her lower legs and feet are missing, and the mummy-makers had given her false ones to make her appear whole. It's a mystery what happened to her, but she might have been bitten by a crocodile, or even a hippo, as she paddled in the river Nile 3000 years ago.

▼ The mummy of Rameses II. Scientific studies have shown that particularly fine linen was used to stuff and bandage the body.

363

A trapped donkey led to the discovery of thousands of mummies! It happened in 1996, when a donkey slipped into a hole at Egypt's Bahariya Oasis. The owner freed it, then climbed down into an underground system of chambers lined with thousands of mummies of ordinary people. The site is called the Valley of the Golden Mummies, as many of the mummies have golden masks over their faces. They are about 2000 years old.

364

Djedmaatesankh – Djed for short – is an Egyptian mummy in the Royal Ontario Museum, Toronto, Canada. She lived around 850 BC, and in 1977 she entered the history books as the first Egyptian mummy to have a whole-body CAT scan (computerized axial tomography). The CAT images revealed that Djed had a serious infection in her jaw, which may have caused her death.

QUIZ

1. What was damaging Rameses II?
2. What is false about Mummy 1770?
3. What did a donkey help to find?
4. Which mummy had the first CAT scan?

Answers:
1. Mould 2. Her legs and feet 3. The Valley of the Golden Mummies 4. Djed

159

Mummies of Peru

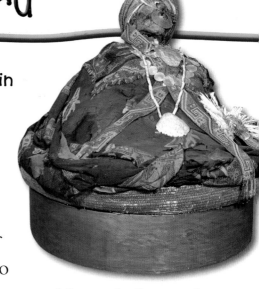

365 Mummies were made in Peru, South America, for hundreds of years. The first were made in the 400s BC, and the last probably in the early 1500s. A body was put into a sitting position, with its knees tucked under its chin. Layers of cloth were wrapped around it to make a 'mummy bundle'. The body was preserved by the dry, cold environment.

▲ This mummy from Peru is more than 500 years old. It was covered in cloth to make a 'mummy bundle'.

366 In the 1500s, the mummies of Inca emperors were paraded through the streets of Cuzco, Peru. People thought that by doing this the souls of the dead were well-cared for, and this helped them on their journey into the afterlife. People also believed that this practice pleased the gods, who then ensured that living people were healthy and happy.

▲ Mummies of emperors were carried through the streets and put on display to the public.

I DON'T BELIEVE IT!

When Spaniards came to Peru in the 1500s, they destroyed thousands of Inca mummies – they got rid of 1365 in just four years!

367

The Incas sacrificed children to their gods. They hoped that in return the gods would provide rain for crops, good health and prosperity. The children's bodies were left at the tops of freezing mountains, where they slowly turned into natural mummies.

368

In 1995, the mummy of a teenage Inca girl was found. She was led to her death 500 years ago, as a sacrifice to the gods. Her body was left 6300 metres up Mount Ampato, Peru, with offerings of cloth, food, gold and silver. The icy conditions preserved her body.

▶ Inca children stand in front of a priest as they prepare to be sacrificed to the gods in a religious ceremony.

Mummies from Asia

369 More than 2500 years ago, the Pazyryk people of Siberia, Russia, buried their leaders in the region's frozen ground. In 1993, a Pazyryk burial mound was dug up, and inside was the frozen mummy of the 'Ice Princess'. She was dressed in clothes made from silk and wool, and she wore a pair of riding boots. When her body thawed from the ice, pictures of deer were found tattooed on her skin.

▲ The Pazyryk people tattooed images of snow leopards, eagles and reindeer onto their bodies. Those found on the 'Ice Princess' may have been a mark of her importance, or rank.

370 Lady Ch'eng is one of the world's best-preserved mummies. She was found in China, and is 2100 years old. Her body had been placed inside a coffin filled with a strange liquid that contained mercury (a silvery liquid metal, also known as quicksilver). The coffin was sealed and placed inside another, and then another. The coffins were buried under a mound of charcoal and clay, and in this watertight, airtight tomb, her body was preserved.

◄ This artist's impression shows how Lady Ch'eng may have looked when she was alive more than 2000 years ago.

372 Vu Khac Minh was a Buddhist monk from Vietnam. In 1639, when he was near the end of his life, he locked himself in his room. He told his fellow monks to leave him alone for 100 days while he meditated (prayed). When this time was up, the monks found that he had died. His body was perfectly preserved and was put on view for all to see.

371 Mummies have been found in China's Taklamakan Desert. It hardly rains here, and the salty sand means that human bodies do not rot. It was a surprise when mummies were found in this remote place. They are about 3000 years old, and look Indo-European, not Chinese. It seems that long ago, a group of tall, light-skinned people settled in the east, where they died and were buried.

◀ Cherchen Man was just one of the many mummies found in the Taklamakan Desert.

North American mummies

373 At 9000 years old, Spirit Cave Man is one of the oldest mummies. The mummy was found in Spirit Cave, Nevada, USA, in 1940. It was wearing a cloak of animal skins, leather moccasins on its feet, and was wrapped inside mats made of tough grass. The cool, dry air in the cave had dried the body, turning it into a natural mummy.

▲ The mummy of Spirit Cave Man. Although it was discovered in 1940, the mummy's actual age was not determined until 1994.

374 The mummy of the North American Iceman no longer exists. It was found in 1999, in Canada. The Iceman had died in the 1400s, and was preserved in a glacier. Native North Americans claimed that the man was their ancestor, so the mummy was handed to them. It was cremated, and the ashes buried near where the mummy had been found.

375 A mummy family was found on Greenland in 1972. The bodies of six Inuit women and two children had been placed on a rocky ledge, in about 1475. The cold conditions had preserved them, slowly freeze-drying their bodies.

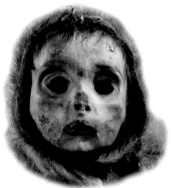

▲ An Inuit mummy of a baby boy. He was killed so that he could stay with his mother in the afterlife.

I DON'T BELIEVE IT!

Hazel Farris, like Elmer McCurdy, was another American outlaw whose mummified body was put on show at funfairs.

377 Elmer McCurdy was an American outlaw who became a mummy! He was shot dead in 1911 after robbing a train. His body was taken to an undertakers where it was preserved, but no one claimed the body. Eventually, McCurdy's mummy was sold to a fairground. In 1976, a TV programme was being filmed at a ghost ride, and a 'dummy' turned out to be the mummy of Elmer McCurdy! He was finally buried in 1977.

376 The mummies of three British sailors lie in the frozen ground of the Arctic. They are John Torrington, John Hartnell and William Braine, who died in 1845 during a voyage from England to find a sea route across the Arctic Ocean. Their bodies were examined in 1984, and it was discovered that they had suffered from lead poisoning, caused by eating contaminated food. The sailors were reburied, and the Arctic began to freeze their bodies again.

▼ The crew of HMS *Terror* try to dig their ship out of the Arctic ice. The men eventually died, and some of their remains were mummified in the freezing conditions.

Worldwide mummies

378 Mount Vesuvius is a volcano in southern Italy. It erupted in AD 79, and the town of Pompeii was buried under a layer of ash and rock. Many people died, mostly by suffocation. As scientists uncovered the town, they found body-shaped areas in the ground. By pouring plaster of Paris into the areas, the shapes of the dead were revealed.

▲ This plaster cast shows a victim of the Vesuvius eruption in AD 79. Some of the casts are so detailed, even facial expressions can be seen.

▼ Fully-dressed mummies line the walls of a church in Palermo, Italy. The dead wished to be preserved wearing their finest clothes.

379 In the underground crypt of a church in Palermo, Sicily, are more than 2000 human mummies. These are the bodies of local people, who were buried in the crypt more than 100 years ago. Instead of rotting away, the dry air has mummified their remains. Many of the mummies are propped against the walls, where they stand at odd angles, dressed in burial clothes.

380

The mummies of saints are displayed in many Roman Catholic churches. It isn't always the whole body that is on show, sometimes it is just a body part, called a 'relic'. Many of the mummies are natural, and are the result of being in a dry environment for many years. A few are artificial, and have been preserved on purpose. However, the Catholic Church believes that some saints have been preserved by God, and are evidence of miracles.

▲ The body of Saint Bernadette Soubirous (1844–1879) at Lourdes, France. Her body was exhumed (dug up) from her grave three times, and had not decomposed. People believed that she had been preserved by God.

381

Mummies have been made on the island of Papua New Guinea for generations. When a person died, they were put into a squatting position and their body was left to dry in the sun, or smoke-dried over a fire. Because the body was preserved, islanders believed their dead relatives were still living with them.

I DON'T BELIEVE IT!

The Guanche people of the Canary Islands, off the coast of West Africa, made mummies until the 1400s.

382

In Japan, there are about 20 mummies of Buddhist priests. The mummy of Tetsumonkai is one of them. He died in 1829, and a few years before his death he started to prepare his body for mummification. He ate less, and stopped eating rice, barley, wheat, beans and millet, as he believed that they harmed the body. After he died, his fellow priests put him in a sitting position with his legs crossed, and then dried out his body.

◄ The mummy of Tetsumonkai. His fellow priests dried his body by placing burning candles around it.

Studying mummies

383 Until recently, mummies were studied by opening them up. Unwrapping Egyptian mummies was popular in the 1800s, and was often done in front of an audience. Thomas Pettigrew (1791–1865) was an English surgeon who unwrapped many mummies at this time. He wrote some of the finest books about Egyptian mummies.

▲ An audience looks on as a mummy is unwrapped in the 1800s. This process destroyed lots of historical evidence.

384 There is no need to open up mummies today. Instead, mummies are studied by taking X-rays of bones, while scans reveal soft tissue in great detail. Mummies can even be tested to work out which families they came from.

▼ A Polish scientist prepares a 3000-year-old Egyptian mummy for an X-ray.

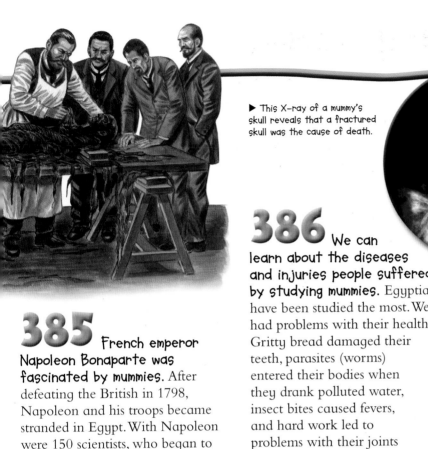

▶ This X-ray of a mummy's skull reveals that a fractured skull was the cause of death.

386 We can learn about the diseases and injuries people suffered by studying mummies.

Egyptian mummies have been studied the most. We can tell they had problems with their health. Gritty bread damaged their teeth, parasites (worms) entered their bodies when they drank polluted water, insect bites caused fevers, and hard work led to problems with their joints and bones.

385 French emperor Napoleon Bonaparte was fascinated by mummies.

After defeating the British in 1798, Napoleon and his troops became stranded in Egypt. With Napoleon were 150 scientists, who began to study Egypt and its mummies.

▼ When Napoleon left Egypt in 1799, he left behind a team of historians and scientists to study Egypt for him.

Animal mummies

387
Animals were mummified in ancient Egypt, too! Birds and fish were mummified as food for a dead person in the next life. Pet cats, dogs and monkeys became mummies so they could keep their dead owners company. Some bulls were believed to be holy as it was thought the spirits of the gods lived inside them. When they died, the bulls were mummified and buried in an underground tomb.

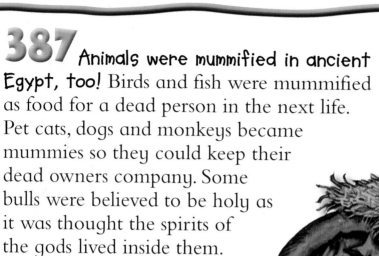

▲ Crocodiles were sacred to the Egyptian god Sobek. They were probably mummified in the same way as humans, then wrapped up.

▼ Fur is still visible around the feet of Dima, the baby mammoth.

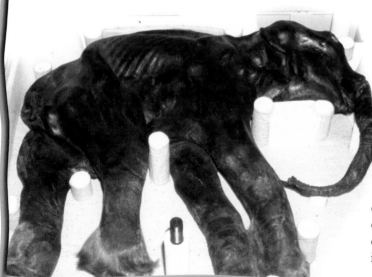

388
A baby mammoth was found in the frozen ground of Siberia in 1977. Many of these ancient elephant-like animals have been found in this part of Russia. What made this one special was the near-perfect state of its body. The animal was about a year old when it died, and was named Dima, after a stream close to where it was discovered.

389 **The world's oldest mummy is a dinosaur!** It is the fossil of an *Edmontosaurus*, which was found in Wyoming, USA, in 1908. This dinosaur died 65 million years ago, but instead of becoming a skeleton, its body was baked dry by the sun. When US fossil hunter Charles Sternberg discovered it, the skin and insides had been fossilized, as well as the bones.

▲ This frog was naturally mummified in 2006 when it died in a plant pot. The sun baked it dry.

390 **Cats have been made into mummies for thousands of years.** In ancient Egypt, cats were linked to the goddess, Bastet. They were bred to be killed as religious offerings at temples. Cat mummies are sometimes found behind the walls of old houses in Europe. It was believed a cat could bring good fortune, so a cat's body was sometimes walled up, after which it dried out until it was a natural mummy.

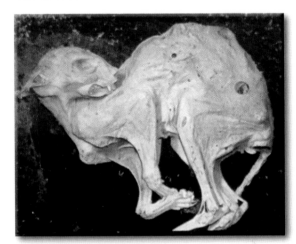

▲ This mummified cat was found in 1971 in Sudbury, Suffolk, UK. It had been walled up in an old mill to protect the building from harm.

Mummy stories

391 The idea of the 'mummy's curse' started in 1923. A letter printed by a London newspaper said people would be cursed if they disturbed any pharaoh's tomb. Tutankhamun's tomb had just been found and people seemed to believe in curses. The letter seemed to confirm their fears. In fact, the entire thing was all made up!

▼ The opening of Tutankhamun's tomb by Howard Carter was the basis for the 'curse of the mummy'.

392 Mummies have not been used to make newspaper! There's a story that says linen was stripped from the mummies of Egypt, then used to make paper. The story goes on to say that an American newspaper was printed on this so-called 'mummy paper', sometime in the 1800s. It's a great story, but it's not true!

393

**A mummy didn't sink *Titanic*
in 1912!** In the British Museum, London, is
the lid of an Egyptian coffin. It is known as
the 'Unlucky Mummy' as it's thought to be
cursed. English journalist William Stead was
on board *Titanic* when it sank. He told a
story about the 'Unlucky Mummy' on the
night the ship sank, and some people
believed that this cursed the voyage.

▼ The 2001 film *The Mummy Returns*
used lots of creepy special effects.

▼ A scene from the 1932 film *The Mummy*.
Boris Karloff played the part of the
mummy character, Im–Ho–Tep (left).

395

**Mummies have become film
stars.** The first mummy film was made
in 1909 and was called *The Mummy of
King Rameses*. It was a black-and-white
film without any sound. Many mummy
films have been made since. One of the
creepiest was *The Mummy*. It was made
in 1932, and starred Boris Karloff.

394

**As long ago as 1827, a
book was written about a mummy.** *The
Mummy! A Tale of the Twenty-second Century*
was written by Jane Loudon. The book
was a science fiction story set in the year
2126. Lots more stories have been written
about mummies since then – some for
children. The author Jacqueline Wilson has
even written *The Cat Mummy*, about a girl
who tries to mummify her dead cat!

QUIZ

1. Was there a mummy on
board *Titanic* ?
2. Which mummy film did
Boris Karloff star in?
3. What started in 1923?
4. Who wrote *The Cat Mummy*?

Answers:
1. No 2. *The Mummy*
3. The mummy's curse
4. Jacqueline Wilson

Modern-day mummies

396 **In Moscow, Russia, and in Beijing, China, modern-day mummies can be found.** When Vladimir Ilich Lenin died in 1924, his body was mummified and put on display in Moscow. The same thing happened in China in 1976, when Mao Zedong died. Both men were leaders of their countries, and after they died, their bodies were preserved so that people could continue to see them.

397 **The wife of a leader was also mummified.** Eva Perón was the wife of the president of Argentina. After her death in 1952, her body was preserved. Then in 1955 the Argentine government was overthrown, and Eva's mummy was sent to Europe. It was returned to Argentina in 1974 to be buried.

▲ The mummy of Lenin is still on display in Moscow, Russia. The body was preserved using a secret technique.

I DON'T BELIEVE IT!

When the British artist Edward Burne-Jones found out that his paint was made from mummy remains, he buried the tube, and put daisies on the 'grave'!

398 **An old man was mummified in America in 1994.** A team of experts became the first people in modern times to mummify a human using ancient Egyptian techniques. They used the same tools as those used by the Egyptian mummy-makers. Then the organs were removed, the body was dried with natron and wrapped in linen.

399 If you have $67,000 (£35,500) to spare, you can have your dead body mummified! Odd as it sounds, there's a company in America that will carry out an Egyptian-style mummification on people. It's cheaper to have a cat or a dog mummified, and the smaller the pet, the less it costs!

400 Modern animal mummies have become works of art. English artist Damien Hirst has taken dead animals such as sheep, cows and sharks and preserved them with a special chemical. They have then been displayed to the public in art galleries as works of art.

▼ This preserved sheep was put on display in London by Damien Hirst in 1994.

The first explorers

401 People have been exploring ever since humans first existed. It is thought that the first humans lived in Africa about two million years ago and then spread out across the world. People probably went exploring to look for food and places to live. Thousands of years ago, seas were shallower, and many places that are now under the sea were dry land. People could walk from Europe to Britain and from Asia to North America. By 10,000 years ago, people had settled all over the world.

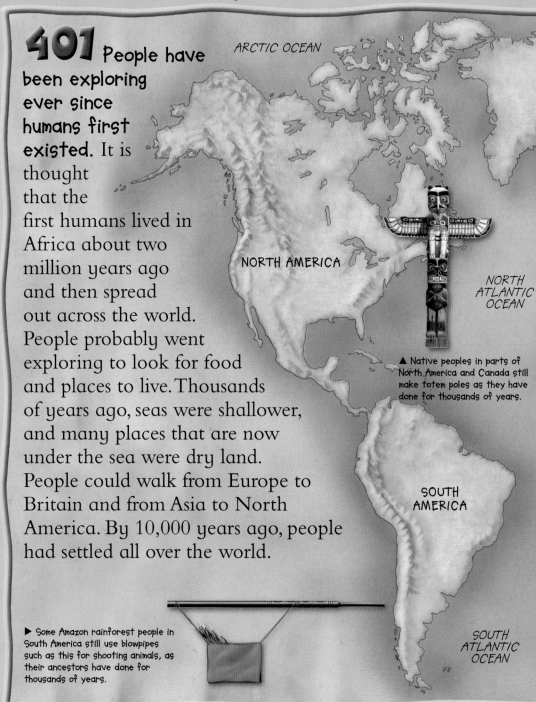

ARCTIC OCEAN

NORTH AMERICA

NORTH ATLANTIC OCEAN

▲ Native peoples in parts of North America and Canada still make totem poles as they have done for thousands of years.

SOUTH AMERICA

SOUTH ATLANTIC OCEAN

▶ Some Amazon rainforest people in South America still use blowpipes such as this for shooting animals, as their ancestors have done for thousands of years.

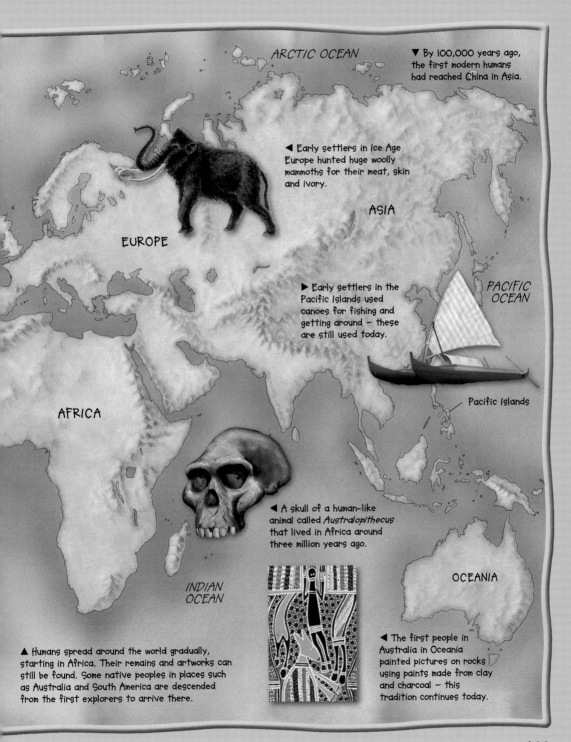

ARCTIC OCEAN

▼ By 100,000 years ago, the first modern humans had reached China in Asia.

◄ Early settlers in Ice Age Europe hunted huge woolly mammoths for their meat, skin and ivory.

ASIA

EUROPE

PACIFIC OCEAN

► Early settlers in the Pacific Islands used canoes for fishing and getting around – these are still used today.

Pacific Islands

AFRICA

◄ A skull of a human-like animal called *Australopithecus* that lived in Africa around three million years ago.

INDIAN OCEAN

OCEANIA

▲ Humans spread around the world gradually, starting in Africa. Their remains and artworks can still be found. Some native peoples in places such as Australia and South America are descended from the first explorers to arrive there.

◄ The first people in Australia in Oceania painted pictures on rocks using paints made from clay and charcoal – this tradition continues today.

177

Ancient adventurers

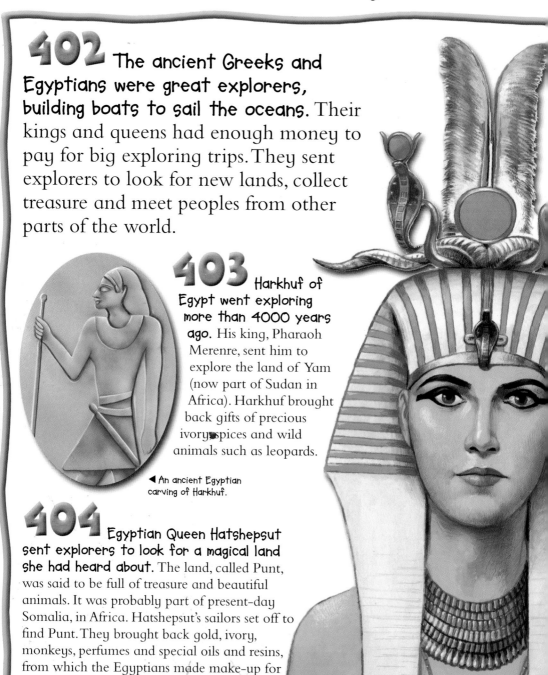

402 The ancient Greeks and Egyptians were great explorers, building boats to sail the oceans. Their kings and queens had enough money to pay for big exploring trips. They sent explorers to look for new lands, collect treasure and meet peoples from other parts of the world.

403 Harkhuf of Egypt went exploring more than 4000 years ago. His king, Pharaoh Merenre, sent him to explore the land of Yam (now part of Sudan in Africa). Harkhuf brought back gifts of precious ivory, spices and wild animals such as leopards.

◀ An ancient Egyptian carving of Harkhuf.

404 Egyptian Queen Hatshepsut sent explorers to look for a magical land she had heard about. The land, called Punt, was said to be full of treasure and beautiful animals. It was probably part of present-day Somalia, in Africa. Hatshepsut's sailors set off to find Punt. They brought back gold, ivory, monkeys, perfumes and special oils and resins, from which the Egyptians made make-up for their faces.

405

In ancient times, the best sailors of all were the Phoenicians (say 'fuh-nee-shuns'). They came from what is now Syria and Lebanon and sailed all over the Mediterranean Sea. In 600 BC, an Egyptian king, Pharaoh Necho II, asked a crew of Phoenicians to see if they could sail all the way around Africa. The trip took them three years. It was 2000 years before anyone sailed around Africa again. The Phoenicians used the stars to help them to navigate (find their way).

▼ For long-distance journeys, the Phoenicians used ships with both sails and oars.

406

Pytheas was an ancient Greek who explored the icy north between 380 and 310 BC. He sailed out of the Mediterranean Sea, past Spain and Britain, and discovered a cold land he named Thule. This might have been Iceland, or part of Norway. Pytheas was the first Greek to see icebergs, the northern lights, and the Sun shining at midnight. However, when he returned to Greece, few people believed his stories.

◄ Hatshepsut stayed at home attending to her duties as queen, while her sailors set off to look for Punt.

I DON'T BELIEVE IT!

When Pytheas sailed past Scotland, he was amazed to see fish the size of boats. In fact they weren't fish at all – they were whales!

Marco Polo

407 Marco Polo is one of the most famous explorers of all time. Marco lived in Venice in Italy in the 1200s and travelled to Asia at a time when most people in Europe never ventured far from their home village. Altogether, Marco travelled more than 40,000 kilometres.

◄ When Marco Polo visited Far Eastern lands such as China, hardly anyone in Europe had ever been there.

◄ This map shows Marco Polo's route across Asia. The journey home took three years.

Venice

CHINA

INDIA

INDIAN OCEAN

408 Marco Polo started exploring when he was just 17 years old. His father and uncle were merchants who went to the Far East on business. When Marco was old enough, they took him with them. In 1271, they all set off for China – a journey that took them three years.

409 In China, the Polos stayed with a mighty emperor called Kublai Khan. He had enormous palaces, rooms full of treasure, and many wives and servants. Kublai Khan gave Marco the job of travelling around his lands to bring him news. Marco went all over China and Southeast Asia.

◄ Coal, fireworks, eyeglasses, ice cream, pasta and paper money were some of the things Marco saw for the first time on his travels.

411 After 20 years away, the Polos were ready to go home. They sailed most of the way in a junk – a Chinese sailing ship. More than 600 passengers and crew died of diseases on the way, but the Polos got home to Venice safely in 1295.

412 Later, there was a war in Italy and Marco Polo was captured. He ended up sharing a prison cell with a writer, and told him his life story. The writer wrote down Marco's travel tales to make a book called *The Travels of Marco Polo*. It became a bestseller!

410 On his travels through Asia, Marco Polo discovered all kinds of amazing inventions. He saw fireworks, coal, paper money, pasta, ice cream and eyeglasses for the first time. He was also impressed to find that the Chinese had a postage system and could post each other letters.

TRUE OR FALSE?

1. In Indonesia, Marco met human beings with tails.
2. A junk is a type of carriage.
3. Christopher Columbus loved reading Marco Polo's book.
4. Marco discovered pizza in China.

Answers:
1. FALSE In his book, Marco said men with tails existed, but he never saw them himself. Now we know it was just an old wives' tale.
2. FALSE It is a type of ship.
3. TRUE Reading Marco Polo's book inspired Columbus to become an explorer.
4. FALSE He discovered pasta, not pizza.

Ibn Battuta

413 **Ibn Battuta became an explorer because of a dream.** Battuta was visiting Mecca, the Muslim holy city, in 1325. There he dreamed that a giant bird picked him up and carried him away. Battuta thought the dream was a message from God, telling him to go exploring. Since he was a Muslim, he decided to visit every Muslim country in the world.

414 **Ibn Battuta set off on his travels, and kept going for nearly 30 years!** He visited more than 40 countries, including present-day Kenya, Iran, Turkey, India and China. Just as he had planned, he visited every Muslim land that existed at the time. Altogether, he travelled more than 120,000 kilometres.

▶ India's Sultan, Muhammad Tughluq, was violent and cruel.

415 **Ibn Battuta stayed in India for seven years, working for the Sultan.** Battuta's job was to be a judge, deciding whether people charged with crimes were innocent or guilty. Battuta was afraid of the Sultan, who was cruel. If anyone disagreed with him, he would have them boiled, beheaded or skinned alive. Once, he nearly beheaded Battuta for being friends with a man he didn't like.

▼ Ibn Battuta's travels began after he dreamed of setting off to the East, carried by a giant bird.

417 Ibn Battuta was lucky to finish his travels alive. During his journey, Battuta was attacked by robbers in India, kept prisoner in the Maldives, chased by pirates in Sri Lanka and shipwrecked several times. At the end of his journey, he saw people suffering from the Black Death, a terrible and deadly disease. Fortunately Battuta managed to avoid catching it.

416 At last, Ibn Battuta went home to Morocco, his own country. When the Sultan heard about his adventures, he asked Battuta to write them all down for him. Battuta didn't have to do the writing himself, though. Instead, he told his story to a scribe (writer) who wrote it all down for him. The finished book was called the *Rihala*, meaning the travels.

I DON'T BELIEVE IT!

In many of the places he visited, Ibn Battuta got married. He had several wives and children in different parts of the world.

Chinese explorers

EUROPE
ASIA
Silk road
CHINA
INDIAN OCEAN

▲ The Silk Road reached across Asia, from Europe to China.

418 Some of the greatest ever explorers came from China. The first was a soldier, Zhang Qian, who lived around 114 BC. The Chinese emporer sent him to find a tribe called the Yueh-Chih, who they hoped would help them fight their enemies, the Huns. On their journey, the Huns captured Zhang Qian and put him in prison for ten years. When he finally escaped and found the Yueh-Chih, they said they didn't want to help!

419 The explorer Xuan Zang was banned from going exploring, but he went anyway. The Chinese emperor wanted him to work in a temple but Xuan Zang wanted to go to India to learn about his religion, Buddhism. In the year 629, he sneaked out of China and followed the Silk Road to Afghanistan. Then he went south to India. Xuan Zang returned 16 years later, with a collection of Buddhist holy books and statues. The emperor was so pleased, he forgave Xuan Zang and gave him a royal welcome.

MAKE A COMPASS

On his travels, Zheng He used a compass to find his way about.

You will need:
magnet   water   large bowl   piece of wood
a real compass

1. Half-fill the large bowl with water.
2. Place the wood in the water with the magnet on top, making sure they do not touch the sides.
3. When the wood is still, the magnet will be pointing to the North and South Poles. You can even check the position with a real compass.

420 By the 1400s, the Chinese were exploring the world. Their best explorer was a sailor named Zheng He. Zheng He used huge Chinese junks to sail right across the Indian Ocean as far as Africa. Wherever he went, Zheng He collected all kinds of precious stones, plants and animals to take back to China to show the emperor. The present that the emperor liked most was a giraffe from East Africa.

◀ The Chinese emperor was thrilled when Zheng He presented him with a live giraffe.

◀ A junk was a giant Chinese sailing ship, bigger than any other ships built at the time.

421 Zheng He's junks were the largest sailing ships on Earth. The biggest was 130 metres long and 60 metres wide. On a typical expedition, Zheng He would take 300 ships and more than 1000 crew members, as well as doctors, map-makers, writers, blacksmiths and gardeners. The gardeners grew fruit and vegetables in pots on the decks, so that there would be plenty of food for everyone.

Sailing around Africa

422 In Europe in the 1400s, people loved spices. They used the strong-tasting seeds and leaves to flavour food and make medicines. Nutmeg, cloves, ginger and pepper came from Asian countries such as India. The spices had to be transported on camels across Asia and Europe, which took a long time. They wanted to find a way to sail from Europe to Asia, to make the journey easier.

Ginger

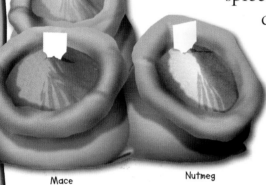

Mace

Nutmeg

423 The best way to sail to Asia was around Africa. But nobody knew how. A Portuguese prince named Henry (1394–1460) started a sailing school to train sailors for the task and began sending ships around the coast of Africa. At first, the sailors were too scared to sail very far because they thought the Atlantic Ocean was too stormy and dangerous. But slowly they sailed further and further.

I DON'T BELIEVE IT!

Sailors were afraid to sail around Africa because of a myth that said if you went too far south in the Atlantic Ocean, the sun would burn you to ashes.

◀ Henry the Navigator never went exploring himself. He just organized expeditions and paid sailors to go on them.

424

In 1488, a captain named Bartolomeu Dias sailed around the bottom of Africa into the Indian Ocean. Dias had a rough journey, so he named the southern tip of Africa The Cape of Storms. It was renamed The Cape of Good Hope to make sailors think it was safe.

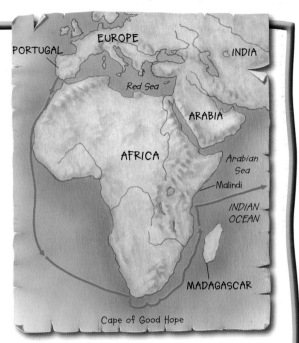

EUROPE
PORTUGAL
INDIA
Red Sea
ARABIA
AFRICA
Arabian Sea
Malindi
INDIAN OCEAN
MADAGASCAR
Cape of Good Hope

▲ Vasco da Gama sailed from Portugal, right around the southern tip of Africa and up the east coast, before crossing the Indian Ocean to India.

425

In 1497, a Portuguese sailor finally sailed around the coast of Africa. His name was Vasco da Gama. After sailing around the Cape of Good Hope, da Gama sailed up the east coast of Africa to Malindi. From there he crossed the Indian Ocean to Calicut in India. Here he hoped to buy spices, but the Rajah, Calicut's ruler, told da Gama he would have to come back with some gold. Da Gama went home empty-handed, but the king of Portugal was very happy. The sea route to Asia had been found, and many traders used it from then on.

◀ Besides being a sea captain, Vasco da Gama was a wealthy nobleman, as his grand outfit shows.

Discovering America

426 **Lots of people think Christopher Columbus discovered America, but he didn't.** The Vikings were the first to sail there, in around the year 1000. They found a land with lots of trees, fish and berries, and called it Vinland. They didn't stay long – they went home after getting into fights with the native Americans. After that, many people forgot that Vinland existed.

▶ The *Santa Maria* was the leader of Columbus' fleet of ships. She was about 23 metres long and had three masts and five sails.

427 **Almost 500 years later, Christopher Columbus found America – by mistake!** Columbus set sail from Spain in 1492, with three ships called the *Santa Maria*, the *Nina* and the *Pinta*. Columbus wasn't looking for a new land. Instead, he wanted to sail right around the Earth to find a new route to Asia, where he planned to buy spices. Although he was Italian, it was Queen Isabella of Spain who gave Columbus money for his trip.

428 When Columbus found land, he was sure he'd sailed to Japan. In fact, Columbus had found the Bahamas, which are close to American mainland.

429 Back in Spain, no one believed Columbus' story. They knew he couldn't have reached China in such a short time. Instead, they realized he must have found a brand new country. People called the new country the New World, and many more explorers set off at once to see it for themselves.

▲ Columbus and two of his men stepping ashore on the Bahamas, to be greeted by the local people.

430 America wasn't named after Columbus. Instead, it was named after another famous explorer, Amerigo Vespucci. In 1507, a map-maker put Amerigo's name on a map of the New World, and changed it from Amerigo to America. The name stuck.

431 It's thanks to Columbus that Native Americans were known as Indians. Since he thought he was in Asia, Columbus called the lands he found the West Indies, and the people he met Indians. They are still called this today – even though America is nowhere near India.

The Conquistadors

432 **'Conquistador' is a Spanish word that means conqueror.** The Conquistadors were Spanish soldiers and noblemen who lived in the 1500s. After Christopher Columbus discovered America in 1492, the Conquistadors set off to explore the new continent. Many of them wanted to get rich by grabbing all the land, gold and jewels they could find in America.

▲ The Aztecs often used the precious stone turquoise in their art. This mask is covered in tiny turquoise tiles.

◀ Leoncico, Balboa's dog, was always at his master's side as he trekked through the forest.

433 **Vasco Nuñez de Balboa was one of the first Conquistadors.** He sailed to America in 1500 to look for treasure. In 1513, Balboa trekked through the jungle with his dog, Leoncico, and an army of soldiers. He was the first European to cross America and see the Pacific Ocean on the other side. Balboa loved his dog so much, he paid him a wage like the soldiers. But like most Conquistadors, Balboa could be cruel too – he killed many local people and stole their gold.

434

Hernan Cortes was a very cunning Conquistador. In 1519, he went to what is now Mexico, to conquer the Aztec people. When he arrived at their city, Tenochtitlan, the people thought he was a god. Cortes captured their king, Montezuma, and took over the city. Montezuma was killed by his own people. Then, after lots of fighting, Cortes took control of the whole Aztec empire.

▼ The Spanish and the Aztecs fought fierce battles, but the Spanish won in the end — mainly because they had guns, and the Aztecs didn't.

435

To conquer the Inca people of Peru, Francisco Pizarro, another explorer, played a nasty trick. In 1532, he captured Atahuallpa, the Inca leader. Atahuallpa said that if Pizarro set him free, he would give him a room filled to the ceiling with gold. Pizarro agreed. But once Atahuallpa had handed over the gold, Pizarro killed him anyway. Then he took over Cuzco, the Inca capital city. Cuzco was high in the mountains, and Pizarro didn't like it. So he started a new capital city at Lima. Today, Lima is the capital city of Peru.

Around the world

▲ Ferdinand Magellan was a clever man who was very good at maths and science. These skills helped him on his exploration.

NORTH AMERICA

Portugo

ATLANTIC OCEAN

PACIFIC OCEAN

SOUTH AMERICA

436 At the start of the 1500s, no one had ever sailed around the world. Portuguese explorer Ferdinand Magellan wanted to sail past South America, and across the Pacific Ocean. It is possible that, like Columbus before him, Magellan thought he could get to Asia that way, where he could buy spices. Then he could sail home past India and Africa – a round-the-world trip.

437 Magellan fell out with the king of Portugal, but the king of Spain agreed to help him. The king paid for five ships and Magellan set off in 1519. Magellan sailed down the coast of South America until he found a way through to the Pacific Ocean. Sailing across the Pacific, many of the crew died from a disease called scurvy. It was caused by not eating enough fresh fruit and vegetables.

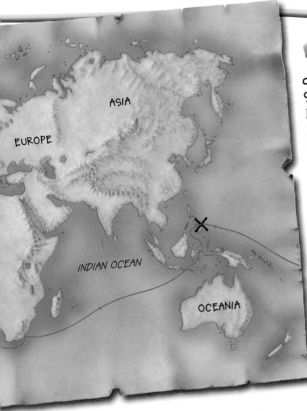

▲ Magellan set off from Spain on his round-the-world trip. X marks the spot where Magellan died, on the island of Mactan.

439 In the end, just one of Magellan's ships made it back to Spain. It picked up a cargo of spices in Indonesia and sailed home. Magellan had taken over 200 crew with him, but less than 20 of them returned. They were the first people to have sailed all the way around the world.

440 Another 55 years went by before anyone sailed around the world again. Queen Elizabeth I asked an English privateer (a kind of pirate) named Francis Drake to try a round-the-world trip in 1577. He made money on the way by robbing Spanish ships (the Queen said he could!). After his three-year voyage, Drake returned to England. Queen Elizabeth gave him a huge reward of £10,000.

438 Magellan made it across the Pacific — but then disaster struck. After landing in the Philippines in 1521, Magellan made friends with the king of the island of Cebu. The king was fighting a war and he wanted Magellan to help him. Magellan and some of his crew went into battle, and Magellan was killed. The rest of the crew took two of the ships and escaped.

QUIZ
Which of these foods would have helped to save Magellan's men from scurvy?

A. Lemon juice
B. Burger in a bun
C. Glass of milk
D. Cabbage
E. Chocolate cake

Answers:
A. and D.

Captain Cook

441 Captain James Cook spent just 11 years exploring, from 1768 to 1779. But he was still one of the greatest explorers. Cook sailed all over the Pacific Ocean and made maps that have helped sailors ever since. He also sailed around the world, north to the Arctic, and south to the Antarctic.

▼ As well as studying the planets, Cook took wildlife experts with him on his explorations. They collected plants that weren't known in Europe, and drew sketches and made notes about them.

Dividers

Pen holder

442 In 1768 the British navy asked Cook to go on an important mission. He was to go to the Pacific island of Tahiti, to make measurements and observations of the planet Venus passing in front of the Sun. After that, Cook went to look for a new continent in the far south – but he didn't find one. Instead, he explored Australia, New Zealand and the Pacific Islands and made new maps.

Parallel ruler

Sector

◄ Cook needed high-quality drawing instruments to help him make his measurements for maps.

443 Many people still believed there was an unknown continent in the south. So they sent Cook back to look for it again in 1772. He sailed further south than anyone had been before, until he found the sea was frozen solid. Cook sailed all the way around Antarctica, but he was never close enough to land to see it. It wasn't explored until 1820, nearly 50 years later.

444 For Cook's third voyage, he headed north. He wanted to see if he could find a sea route between the Pacific Ocean and the Atlantic Ocean, across the top of Canada. After searching for it in 1778, he went to spend the winter in Hawaii. At first, the Hawaiians thought Cook was a god named Lono!

I DON'T BELIEVE IT!

Captain Cook was the first European to discover Hawaii, in 1778. He called it the Sandwich Islands.

445 Cook found his way around better than any sailor before him. An inventor named John Harrison had created a new clock (called the chronometer) that could measure the time precisely, even at sea. Before that, clocks had pendulums, so they didn't work on ships. From the time that the sun went down, Cook could work out exactly how far east or west he was.

▼ An early chronometer, invented by John Harrison.

Crossing America

446 **The United States of America was created in 1776 — less than 250 years ago.** At that time, there were huge parts of it that still hadn't been explored. In 1803, the third president of the USA, Thomas Jefferson, asked Meriwether Lewis to go exploring. Lewis asked his friend William Clark to go with him.

▼ After the Missouri grew too narrow for their boat, Lewis and Clark's team used canoes. Local Native American guides helped them to paddle and find their way.

447 **Lewis and Clark planned to travel all the way across America to the Pacific Ocean.** They built a special boat for sailing on rivers. The boat could be rowed, pushed along with a pole, or towed with a rope. It also had sails for catching the wind. They took a crew of about 40 men, and in May 1804, they set off from the city of St Louis, sailing along the Missouri River.

▶ It's thought that Sacagawea died a few years after the Lewis and Clark expedition, aged just 25 or 26.

448 **In North Dakota, Lewis and Clark made a new friend — Sacagawea.** She was a Shoshone Native American who joined the expedition as a guide. She helped Lewis and Clark to make friends with the Native American peoples they met during their trip. She knew where to find plants that they could eat and how to make tools. She also saved a pile of valuable papers that were about to fall into the river.

449
During the trip, Lewis and Clark were scared by bears. One day, Lewis was out hunting when a grizzly bear chased him. Lewis tried to shoot it, but he was out of bullets. The bear chased him into a river, but Lewis was in luck – the bear changed its mind and walked away.

MAKE A TOTEM POLE
You will need:
scissors   cardboard tube   paper
felt-tip pens   glue

1. Cut strips of paper long enough to wrap around the tube.
2. Draw faces, monsters and birds on the strips, then glue them around the tube.
3. Make wings from paper and glue them to the back of the tube.
4. Make a beak by cutting out a triangle, folding it in half and gluing it to the front of the tube.

451
The crew paddled in canoes along the Columbia River to the sea. They reached the Pacific Ocean in November 1805 – then turned around and trekked all the way back. When they got home, Lewis and Clark were national heroes. The president gave them money and land.

450
As they crossed the Rocky Mountains, Lewis and Clark and their men almost starved. They couldn't find any buffalo or deer to hunt and eat, so they had to eat three of their own horses. They were only saved when they met a group of Nez Perce Native Americans who gave them food.

▶ Lewis and Clark were in danger of getting badly lost in the Rocky Mountains. Locals showed them the way and gave them food, which saved their lives.

Exploring Africa

452 **When Europeans began exploring Africa, they found it could be deadly.** In 1795, Scottish doctor Mungo Park went to explore the Niger River, in West Africa. Along the way, Park was robbed, kept prisoner, had all his clothes stolen, almost died of thirst and fell ill with a fever. However, he still went back to Africa in 1805.

Mungo Park

▶ Livingstone made many of his journeys by boat. On one occasion, his boat collided with a hippo and overturned, causing him to lose some of his equipment.

453 **Dr David Livingstone was one of the most famous explorers of Africa.** He went there in 1840 as a missionary, to try to teach African people to be Christians. He trekked right across the dusty Kalahari Desert with his wife and young children and discovered Lake Ngami. He was also mauled by a lion, so badly that he could never use his left arm again.

455 Dr Livingstone kept exploring and became the first European to travel all the way across Africa. On the way, he discovered a huge, beautiful waterfall on the Zambezi River. The locals called it Mosi Oa Tunya, meaning 'the smoke that thunders'. Livingstone renamed it Victoria Falls, after Britain's Queen Victoria.

456 In 1869, Dr Livingstone went missing. He had gone exploring in East Africa and no one had heard from him. Everyone thought he had died. An American writer, Henry Stanley, went to look for Livingstone. He found him in the town of Ujiji, in Tanzania. He greeted him with the words: "Dr Livingstone, I presume?"

▼ It took Henry Stanley eight months to find Dr Livingstone in Africa.

▲ At their centre, the Victoria Falls are 108 metres high.

454 French explorer René Caillié went exploring in disguise. He wanted to see the ancient city of Timbuktu in the Sahara Desert, but only Muslims were allowed in. He dressed up as an Arab trader and sneaked into the city in 1828. He was the first European to go there and return home alive.

The source of the Nile

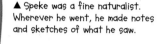

457 **In the ancient world, the Nile was an important river.** It provided the Egyptians with water, and the Greeks and Romans knew about it, too. Ancient explorers tried to sail up the Nile to see where it went, but they kept getting stuck. An Egyptian named Ptolemy drew a map of the Nile, showing it flowing from a big lake in the middle of Africa.

▲ Speke was a fine naturalist. Wherever he went, he made notes and sketches of what he saw.

458 **In the 1800s, explorers still wanted to find the beginning, or 'source', of the Nile.** In 1856, two British explorers named Richard Burton and John Speke set off to find it. They trekked across Africa to look for the big lake. Both men soon caught the disease malaria from mosquito bites. Burton became so ill he had to stop and rest.

▲ Richard Burton was an English army officer who learned to speak 29 languages.

▲ The Nile is the world's longest river. It flows across the entire length of the desert lands of Egypt.

▶ As it turned out, Ptolemy was right. The Nile does flow from a great lake in the middle of Africa – Lake Victoria.

AFRICA

Lake Victoria

Lake Victoria

Nile River

INDIAN OCEAN

Lake Tanganyika

459 Speke continued on and discovered a huge lake, which he named Lake Victoria. He was sure it was the source of the Nile. He returned to Britain and told everyone he had found the source. Burton was furious. Speke went back to Africa to explore the lake, and found the place where the Nile flows out of it.

460 Meanwhile, two other explorers were sailing up the Nile to find the source. They were a married couple, Samuel and Florence White Baker. In 1864, they had sailed so far up the Nile that they met Speke coming the other way. The mystery of where the Nile began had been solved once and for all.

Exploring Australia

▶ The didgeridoo is a traditional musical instrument made from a hollowed out tree trunk. It is an important part of the historical culture of the aboriginal people.

461
People settled in Australia more than 50,000 years ago. The aboriginal people have lived there ever since. Just 400 years ago, in the early 1600s, sailors from Europe began to explore Australia. Britain claimed Australia for itself, and lots of British people went to live there.

462
European settlers were sure there was a huge sea in the middle of Australia. In 1844, a soldier named Charles Sturt went to look for the sea. He found that the middle of Australia was a hot, dry desert (now called the outback). His men got sunburn and scurvy, and their fingernails crumbled to dust. Sturt himself nearly went blind. But he had proved the mythical sea did not exist.

▼ Burke and Wills took more than 40 horses and camels on their expedition. The camels were from India, as they were well suited to Australia's dry climate.

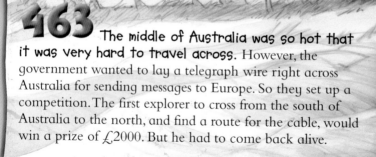

463
The middle of Australia was so hot that it was very hard to travel across. However, the government wanted to lay a telegraph wire right across Australia for sending messages to Europe. So they set up a competition. The first explorer to cross from the south of Australia to the north, and find a route for the cable, would win a prize of £2000. But he had to come back alive.

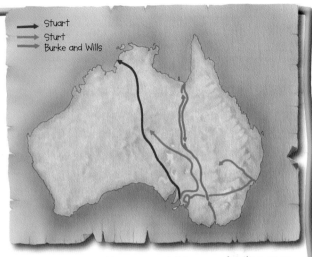

Stuart
Sturt
Burke and Wills

464 Irishman Robert Burke decided to try for the prize. He set off in 1860 with a team of horses and camels. Four men – Burke, William Wills, and two others – made it all the way across Australia. On the way back one man died, and they stopped to bury him. The rest of the team, waiting to meet them, gave up and went home. The three survivors were left alone in the desert, and Burke and Wills starved to death. Only one man lived – he was rescued by Aborigines.

▲ Only Stuart's expedition was completely successful. His journey opened up the interior of Australia for settlement and farming.

465 Meanwhile, another explorer was racing Burke for the prize. John McDouall Stuart took a different route across Australia, further west than Burke's. Unlike Burke, Stuart made it back alive – but he almost died. When he came home to Adelaide to claim his prize, he was so sick he had to be carried on a stretcher.

QUIZ

The Aborigines could survive in the outback because they knew what foods to eat and where to find them. Which of these foods could Burke's men have eaten?
1. Bunya nut
2. Wichetty grub (a kind of baby insect)
3. Seaweed
4. Ostrich eggs
5. Wild honey

Answers:
1, 2 and 5. Not ostrich eggs, as ostriches are only found in Africa. Not seaweed, as it is only found in the sea.

Arctic adventures

466 **The Arctic is the land and sea around the North Pole.** Explorers first went there to search for the Northwest Passage – the sea-route leading from the Atlantic Ocean to the Pacific Ocean. They spent 400 years trying to find it, and many explorers died of cold or drowned in the Arctic Ocean.

467 **Norwegian explorer Roald Amundsen was the first to sail through the Northwest Passage.** Amundsen used a small fishing boat that made it easier to sail along shallow channels and between chunks of floating ice. But the journey still took him three years – from 1903 to 1906. Amundsen learned a lot about surviving in the cold from local peoples he met on the way.

468 **There was still part of the Arctic where no one had been – the North Pole.** Another Norwegian explorer, Fridtjof Nansen, built a ship called the *Fram*, which was designed to get stuck in the ice without being damaged. As the ice moved, it carried the *Fram* nearer to the Pole. Nansen almost reached the Pole in 1895 – but not quite.

469 Next, an American named Robert Peary and his assistant Matthew Henson, set off for the North Pole. Peary had always wanted to be the first to get there. After two failed attempts, Peary used dogsleds and Inuit guides to help him reach the pole in the year 1909.

470 When Peary announced that he had been to the Pole, he was in for a shock. Another explorer, Frederick Cook, who had been Peary's friend, said he had got there first! The two men had an argument. Then it was revealed that Cook had lied about another expedition. After that, nobody believed he had been to the North Pole either.

▲ Peary and Henson used traditional sealskin clothes for their journey, and paid local Inuit people to make their clothes and equipment.

◄ Fridtjof Nansen's boat, the *Fram*, was specially shaped so that when it was squeezed by ice, it lifted up instead of getting crushed. This allowed the ship to move safely with the ice towards the North Pole.

I DON'T BELIEVE IT!

Some experts think Peary didn't actually reach the North Pole. If this is true then the first person at the North Pole was Wally Herbert, who walked there in 1969.

Antarctic adventures

471 **Antarctica was explored less than 200 years ago.** This large and mountainous continent is at the southern tip of the Earth. It is even colder than the Arctic and very dangerous. In the early 1900s, explorers such as Robert Scott and Ernest Shackleton tried to reach the South Pole and failed. In 1909, Shackleton came within 155 kilometres of the South Pole, but had to turn back.

▶ Amundsen's team used lightweight dogsleds. If a dog died or became too weak to go on, it was fed to the other dogs. This reduced the amount of food the men had to carry.

472 **In 1910, British explorer Robert Scott decided to set off for the South Pole again.** He took motor sleds and ponies to carry all his supplies. He decided that when his men got near the Pole, they would pull their own sleds. In Antarctica, he also wanted to collect rock samples to study.

473 **Meanwhile, Roald Amundsen was on his way to try to reach the North Pole.** But when he heard that Robert Peary had already got there, he decided to race Scott to the South Pole instead. Amundsen used different methods from Scott – sleds pulled by husky dogs carried supplies.

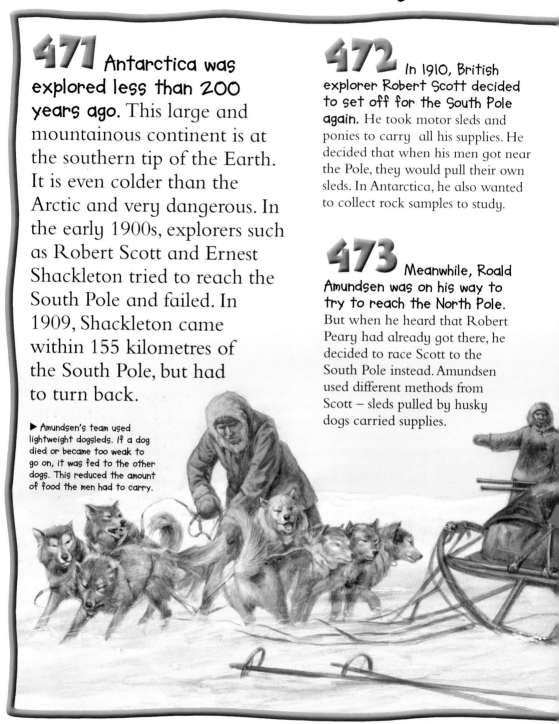

474 In 1911, both Scott and Amundsen reached Antarctica, and set off for the South Pole. Amundsen left first and got there quickly with his dogs. Scott's motor sleds broke down and his ponies died. His team trudged to the Pole, only to find Amundsen had been there first. On the way back, Scott's men got stuck in a blizzard. They ran out of food, and died of cold and hunger.

▲ When Scott's team reached the South Pole, they took photos of each other, but their faces showed how upset they were not to be there first.

475 Shackleton never got to the South Pole – but he had a very exciting Antarctic adventure. He wanted to trek across Antarctica in 1914. But before he could start, his ship, the *Endurance*, was crushed by the ice. The crew were left on the frozen ocean with just three lifeboats. Shackleton left his men on an island while he took one tiny boat to get help. He had to cross a stormy ocean and climb over icy mountains before he found a village. All his men were rescued and came home safely.

Scientific searches

476 **Lots of great explorers were scientists.** Some went exploring to find rocks and minerals, or to study mountains or seas. Some were looking for new species (types) of plants and animals. Today, scientists explore in jungles, deserts and oceans to look for things no one else has found before.

▲ Darwin studied the many different types of finch on the Galapagos Islands.

▲ Darwin made notes about his findings. He believed that plants and animals changed to suit their surroundings.

477 **Charles Darwin went on a round-the-world voyage on a ship called the _Beagle_, from 1831 to 1836.** As the ship's naturalist (nature expert), it was Darwin's job to collect new species. He found all kinds of birds, plants, lizards, insects and other living things. He found many strange fossils, too. Back in England, Darwin wrote lots of important books about the natural world.

▼ The horses we know today developed gradually from smaller horselike animals over a period of about 55 million years. Darwin called this process of gradual change evolution.

Eohippus

Mesohippus

Parahippus

Merychippus

Pliohippus

Equus

478 Henry Bates' favourite animals were bugs.
In 1848, Bates went to the Amazon rainforest to study butterflies, beetles and other insects. He found more than 8000 species that no one had known about before. He also discovered that some harmless animals look like poisonous animals to stay safe. Today, this is called 'Batesian mimicry' (mimicry means copying).

◀ The hornet moth is an example of 'Batesian mimicry'. It is harmless but it mimics the hornet, which has a painful sting. This helps to scare predators away.

Hornet moth

Hornet

TRUE OR FALSE?

1. Henry Bates discovered more than 8000 species of insects.
2. Aimé Bonpland was an expert on local medicines.
3. Darwin's ship was called the *Basset*.
4. Mary Kingsley became caught in an animal trap.

Answers:
1.TRUE 2.FALSE Aimé Bonpland was a plant-expert.
3. FALSE Darwin's ship was called the *Beagle*. 4.TRUE

479 German scientist Alexander von Humboldt wanted to understand everything in the world.
He and his friend, French plant-expert Aimé Bonpland, explored South America for five years between 1799 and 1804. They studied all kinds of things – poisonous plants, local medicines, ocean currents, rocks, rivers, mountains, and the stars at night. Later, Humboldt wrote a book, *Kosmos*, all about nature.

▶ Von Humboldt studied landscape extensively. The cold sea current that flows up the west coast of South America is named in his honour.

480 Mary Kingsley loved exploring rivers in Africa.
She searched for new species – especially river fish – and studied the way of life of local rainforest people. On her travels, Kingsley fell into an animal trap full of spikes, got caught in a tornado, was cornered by an angry hippo and had a crocodile climb into her canoe.

Archaeological adventures

▲ The Nabataean people built many beautiful temples on the small plain at Petra.

481 Old ruined cities, palaces and tombs can stay hidden for centuries. Some get buried or covered with desert sand. Some are in faraway places where no one goes any more. When an explorer finds an ancient ruin, it can reveal lots of secrets about how people used to live long ago. Finding things out from ancient ruins is called archaeology.

482 Swiss explorer Johann Ludwig Burckhardt wanted to explore Africa. First he went to the Middle East to learn Arabic for his African trip. In 1812, in what is now Jordan, he discovered an amazing ruined city, carved out of red and yellow rock. It was Petra, the capital of the Nabataean people, built in the 2nd century. Burckhardt was the first European to go there.

483
The city of Troy, which you can read about in the Greek myths, really existed. In 1870, German archaeologist Heinrich Schliemann travelled to Turkey to see if he could find Troy. He discovered the ruins of nine cities, one of which he thought was Troy. He found it had been destroyed and rebuilt many times. Schliemann also dug up piles of beautiful gold jewellery from the ruins.

484
In 1911, American explorer Hiram Bingham found a lost city, high on a mountain in Peru. The local people knew about it, and called it Machu Picchu, meaning 'old mountain', but the outside world had no idea it was there. Bingham wrote a book about his discovery, and today, half a million tourists visit it every year.

◄ Schliemann's wife, Sophia, wearing some of the jewels found in the ruins uncovered by her husband.

▲ The cave paintings at Lascaux depict animals such as bison, deer and horses.

MAKE A CAVE PAINTING

You will need:
paper (rough beige paper looks best)
red and black paint   twigs
To make your painting look like real Lascaux cave art, use a twig dipped in paint to draw stick figures and animals such as cows, deer and cats. You can also try making patterns of spots using your fingertips.

485
Four teenagers exploring a cave stumbled upon some of the world's most important cave paintings. The cave was in Lascaux, France, and the four boys found it in 1940, after a tree fell down, leaving a hole in the ground. Inside were passages leading to several rooms. The walls were covered with paintings of wild animals and humans who had lived 17,000 years ago.

The highest mountains

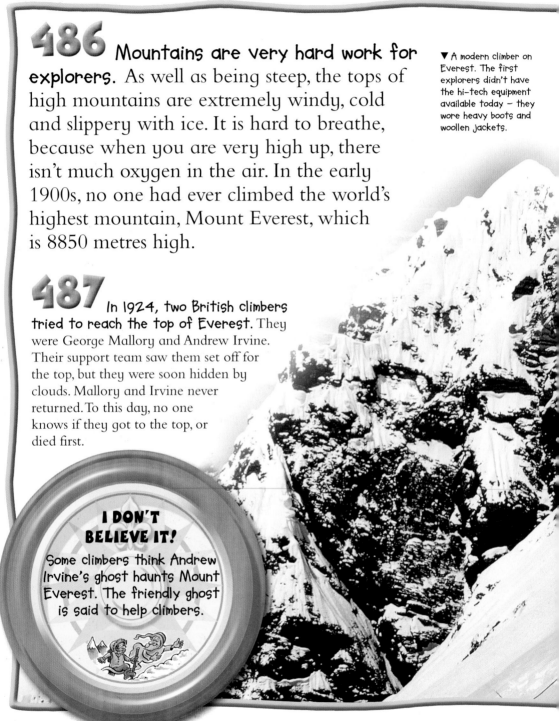

486 **Mountains are very hard work for explorers.** As well as being steep, the tops of high mountains are extremely windy, cold and slippery with ice. It is hard to breathe, because when you are very high up, there isn't much oxygen in the air. In the early 1900s, no one had ever climbed the world's highest mountain, Mount Everest, which is 8850 metres high.

▼ A modern climber on Everest. The first explorers didn't have the hi-tech equipment available today – they wore heavy boots and woollen jackets.

487 **In 1924, two British climbers tried to reach the top of Everest.** They were George Mallory and Andrew Irvine. Their support team saw them set off for the top, but they were soon hidden by clouds. Mallory and Irvine never returned. To this day, no one knows if they got to the top, or died first.

I DON'T BELIEVE IT!

Some climbers think Andrew Irvine's ghost haunts Mount Everest. The friendly ghost is said to help climbers.

488
In the 1950s, many countries were trying to send climbers to the top of Everest. A Swiss expedition nearly made it in 1952. In 1953, a British team set off. Two climbers, Evans and Bourdillon, climbed to within 90 metres of the summit, but had to turn back when an oxygen tank broke. Then, another two climbers tried. Their names were Edmund Hillary and Tenzing Norgay.

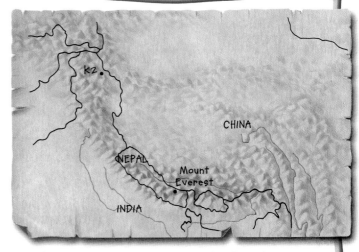

▲ Hillary and Norgay started their approach to Everest from its south side – which had been called unclimbable.

489
At 11.30 a.m. on 28 May, 1953, Tenzing and Hillary stood on top of Mount Everest. They hugged each other and took photos. They couldn't stay long, as they had to get back to their camp before their oxygen ran out. Hillary and Tenzing made it home safely, but many people have died trying to come back down Mount Everest after reaching the top.

490
There was still a mighty mountain yet to be climbed. K2, the world's second-highest mountain, is even more dangerous than Everest. People had been trying to climb it since 1902, and many had died. At last, in 1954, an Italian team succeeded. Lino Lacedelli and Achille Compagnoni were chosen to go to the top. Their oxygen ran out, but they kept going and reached the summit.

Under the sea

491 In 1872, a ship set out to explore a new world – the bottom of the sea. But the HMS *Challenger* wasn't a submarine. It measured the seabed, using ropes to find out the depth of the ocean. On its round-the-world voyage, *Challenger's* crew also found many new species of sea creatures.

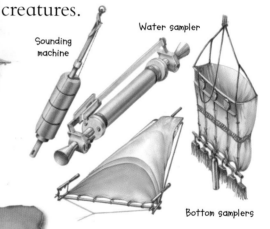

Sounding machine

Water sampler

Bottom samplers

▲ HMS *Challenger* and some of the equipment her crew used to measure the shape and depth of the seabed all around the world.

TRUE OR FALSE?

1. The HMS *Challenger* was a submarine.
2. William Beebe was a wildlife specialist.
3. Beebe and Barton dived down into the Indian Ocean.
4. Scientists think that there are many new sea creatures that have not yet been discovered.

Answers:
1. FALSE It was a ship. 2. TRUE 3. FALSE Beebe and Barton dived down into the Atlantic Ocean. 4. TRUE

492 Lots of people still wanted to explore the seabed themselves. In 1928, an engineer, Otis Barton, and a wildlife professor, Wiliam Beebe, built the bathysphere, a round steel ball that could be lowered into the sea. In 1934, Beebe and Barton climbed inside and dived 923 metres down into the Atlantic Ocean.

493 Another inventor, Auguste Piccard, invented a craft called the bathyscaphe. It wasn't lowered from a ship, but could travel about by itself. In 1960, a bathyscaphe named *Trieste* took two passengers to the deepest part of the sea, Challenger Deep, in the Pacific Ocean. It is more than 10,900 metres deep.

▼ Chimney-shaped hydrothermal vents surrounded by giant tubeworms, which can grow more than one metre long.

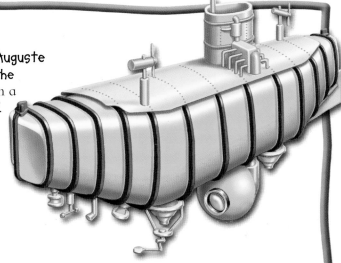

▲ The *Trieste*'s two passengers crouched inside the round part that you can see hanging below the main section.

494 In 1977, scientists discovered strange chimneys on the seabed and named them hydrothermal vents. Hot water from inside the Earth flowed out of these vents. The hot water contained minerals that living things could feed on. All around the vents were weird sea creatures that no one had ever seen before, such as giant tubeworms and giant clams.

495 The seas and oceans are so big, that parts of the undersea world are still unknown. There could be all kinds of strange sea caves and underwater objects we haven't found. Scientists think there could also be many new sea creatures, such as giant squid, sharks and whales, still waiting to be discovered.

496 There's still one place humans have hardly explored at all, and that's space. Space exploration started in October 1957, when *Sputnik I*, a Russian spacecraft, was launched. A rocket sent *Sputnik* into orbit around the Earth. But this first spacecraft had no passengers.

▼ Laika the space dog was a half-husky mongrel.

497 The first-ever astronaut went into space the same year. She wasn't a human, but a dog named Laika. She went into space aboard another Russian spacecraft, *Sputnik II*, in November 1957. Sadly, Laika died during the voyage, but she led the way for human space exploration.

▼ Yuri Gagarin in his spacesuit, shortly before leaving the planet to become the first ever human in space.

498 In 1961, Yuri Gagarin became the first human to go into space. His spacecraft was called *Vostok I*. After going into orbit, Gagarin flew once around the Earth, which took nearly two hours. Then *Vostok I* came back down to Earth, and landed safely. Gagarin's trip proved people could travel in space.

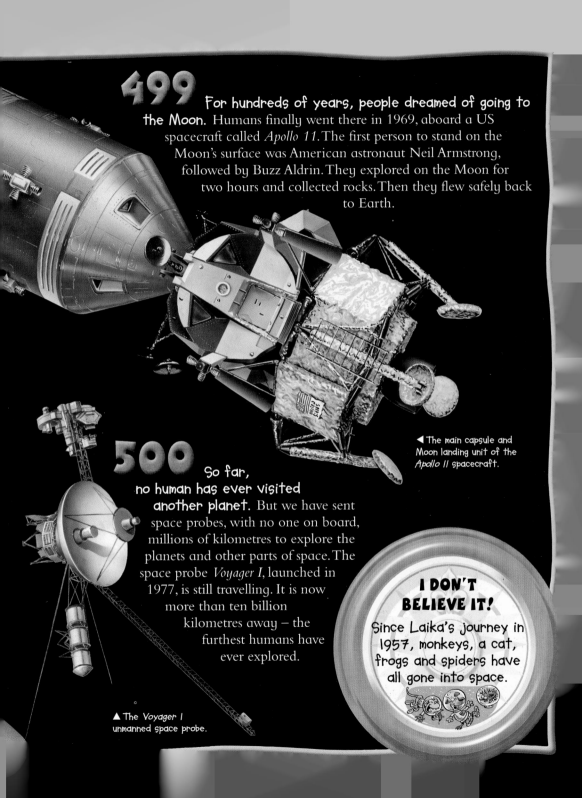

499 For hundreds of years, people dreamed of going to the Moon. Humans finally went there in 1969, aboard a US spacecraft called *Apollo 11*. The first person to stand on the Moon's surface was American astronaut Neil Armstrong, followed by Buzz Aldrin. They explored on the Moon for two hours and collected rocks. Then they flew safely back to Earth.

◀ The main capsule and Moon landing unit of the *Apollo II* spacecraft.

500 So far, no human has ever visited another planet. But we have sent space probes, with no one on board, millions of kilometres to explore the planets and other parts of space. The space probe *Voyager I*, launched in 1977, is still travelling. It is now more than ten billion kilometres away – the furthest humans have ever explored.

▲ The *Voyager I* unmanned space probe.

I DON'T BELIEVE IT!

Since Laika's journey in 1957, monkeys, a cat, frogs and spiders have all gone into space.

Index

Entries in **bold** refer
to main subject entries.
Entries in *italics* refer
to illustrations.

Index

Index

Acknowledgements

The publishers would like to thank the following sources for the use of their photographs:

Alamy 35 Charles Stirling (Diving)

The Art Archive 210(t)

Corbis 92–93 Bettmann; 100–101 Bettmann; 128 Roger Wood; 130 K M Westermann; 140 Christophe Boisvieux; 168(b) Remigiusz Sikora/epa; 200–201; 212–213

The Greenland Museum 164(b) Werner Forman Archive

John Malam 171(c)

Photolibrary Group LTD 141(t)

Pictorial Press 129 Dreamworks/Universal; 131 Bryna/Universal; 132 Dreamworks/Universal

Rex Features 41 KPA/Zuma

TopFoto.co.uk 32 2004 Topham Picturepoint; 38–39; 142 Topham Picturepoint; 144–145 The British Museum/HIP; 156; 157(t) Topham Picturepoint; 160(t) Topham Picturepoint; 166(t) Topham Picturepoint, (b) Charles Walker; 167(c) Fortean/Trottmann; 169(t) Charles Walker, (b) Rogér-Viollet; 170(b); 171(b) TopFoto/Fotean; 172 Topham Picturepoint; 173(t) Topham Picturepoint, (c) TopFoto/HIP; 174–175(c) RIA Novosti; 175(b) Topham Picturepoint

All other images from the Miles Kelly Archives